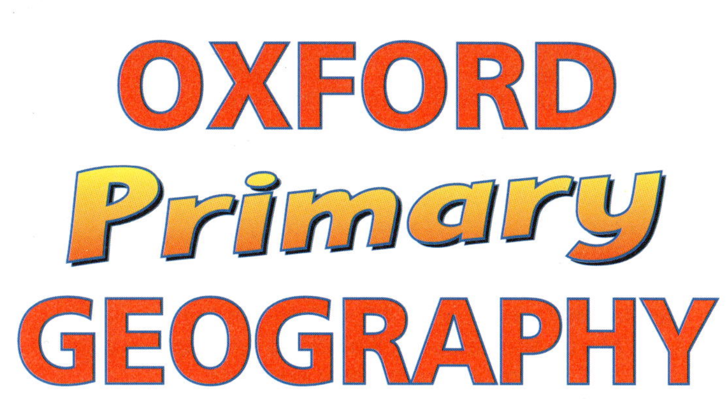
OXFORD
Primary
GEOGRAPHY

Series Consultant Steve Harrison

4

Simon Asquith Pam Jervis
John Lancaster Lynn Lancaster Heather Starkie

OXFORD

The publishers would like to thank the following for permission to reproduce photographs:

Camera Press: p 10 top; Comstock Photo Library: pp 20 middle, 21 top, 26 bottom right, 43; Environmental Picture Library: p 22 top; Greg Evans International: pp 9 bottom left, 10 bottom, 13 top left and bottom right, 20 bottom right; Eunice Gill: p 42 right; London Regional Transport (LRT Registered User No. 95/2248): p 11 middle; London Transport Museum: pp 9 bottom right, 13 bottom left; The Mansell Collection: pp 4/5; Q A Photos Ltd: p 7 top; Rex Features Ltd: pp 17, 35; Martin Sookias: pp 6, 8 all, 9 top left, top right and middle right, 13 top right; Still Pictures Environmental Agency: p 22 bottom; Telegraph Colour Library: p 9 middle; Port of Tilbury, London: p 7 bottom; Zefa Pictures: p 11 top.

The front cover picture was by Tony Stone Images.

All other images are courtesy of the authors.

Illustrations by Tony Morris and Oxford Illustrators.
Maps by Jeff Edwards.

Oxford University Press, Walton Street, Oxford OX2 6DP

Oxford New York
Athens Auckland Bangkok Bombay
Calcutta Cape Town Dar es Salaam Delhi
Florence Hong Kong Istanbul Karachi
Kuala Lumpur Madras Madrid Melbourne
Mexico City Nairobi Paris Singapore
Taipei Tokyo Toronto

and associated companies in
Berlin and *Ibadan*

ISBN 0 19 833473 7

Printed in Hong Kong

Contents

LONDON
THE RHINE
KENYA
PEOPLE AND THE ENVIRONMENT
WORLD TRAVELLER

London: an historic city

London has been an important city since Roman times.

Ships could sail up the Thames as far as London, where the river could be bridged.

The picture shows London in 1616. This was before the Great Fire of London.

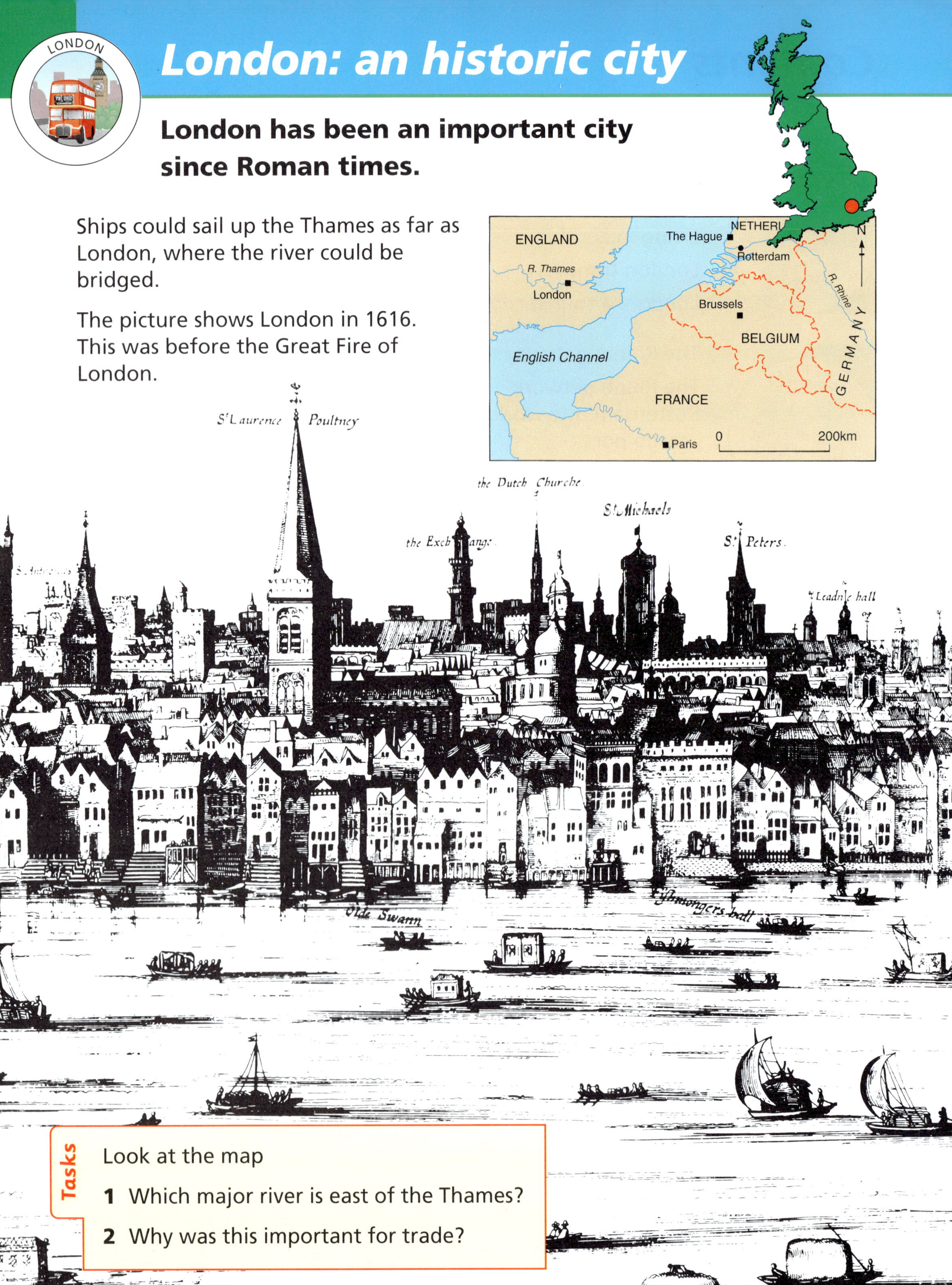
LONDON
ENGLAND
R. Thames
London
English Channel
The Hague
Rotterdam
Brussels
BELGIUM
FRANCE
Paris
R. Rhine
GERMANY
N
0
200km
S.t Laurence Poultney
the Dutch Churche
S.t Michaels
the Exchange
S.t Peters
Olde Swann

Tasks

Look at the map

1 Which major river is east of the Thames?

2 Why was this important for trade?

Tasks

Look at the picture

3 How many churches are named?

4 How many types of boat can you see on the river?

5 What was each type used for?

6 How did a sail boat pass under the bridge?

7 Why were there steps down to the river?

8 How many bridges crossed the river?

9 Describe the buildings on the bridge.

10 Do you know of any bridges today with buildings on them?

11 How did people cross the river?

12 Could the countryside be seen from the bridge in
a) 1616 b) today?

St. Dunston in the east
St. Hellen
St. Andrew
Billins gate
THE BRIDGE

By Nicholas John Visscher
Amsterdam 1616
Mansell Collection

LONDON

Travelling to London

London, as the capital city, needs good communication links with the rest of Britain and the wider world.

N
Key
Motorways
Major roads
Railways
Inverness
Aberdeen
A94
Glasgow
Edinburgh
M74
A74
A1
Newcastle
M6
A1
Leeds
Hull
Liverpool
Holyhead
Manchester
A5
M1
M6
A1
A11
Birmingham
Fishguard
A40
M40
M1
M11
Ipswich
London
Cardiff
Bristol
M4
M5
M3
M20
Dover
Exeter
Southampton
Plymouth
0
100km

This map shows the motorways, main roads and railways to London.

	Aberdeen	Birmingham	Bristol	Cardiff	Dover	Edinburgh	Hull	Leeds	Liverpool	Manchester	Newcastle	Southampton
London	787	176	186	245	115	597	269	304	315	294	437	123
Aberdeen		648	774	781	894	190	546	496	528	526	360	848
Birmingham			139	163	291	458	198	174	144	126	320	205
Bristol				69	299	584	325	310	256	254	454	120
Cardiff					360	589	360	333	262	275	477	184
Dover						704	378	411	430	408	544	222
Edinburgh							355	306	336	336	170	658
Hull								88	205	149	187	403
Leeds									117	64	146	358
Liverpool										56	245	346
Manchester											205	330
Newcastle												498

This chart shows the distances in kilometres between London and some other British towns and cities.

INTERCI
43090

Tasks

1 Describe the routes (roads and motorways) to London from the following places

a) Manchester,
b) Cardiff,
c) Aberdeen.

2 Use the chart to help you find the distance to London from

a) Leeds,
b) Bristol,
c) Birmingham,
d) Hull.

3 There are two main rail lines from London to Scotland. List the cities linked by the eastern line and those linked by the western line.

4 Use an atlas to find which large towns are avoided by using the M1 from Leeds to London.

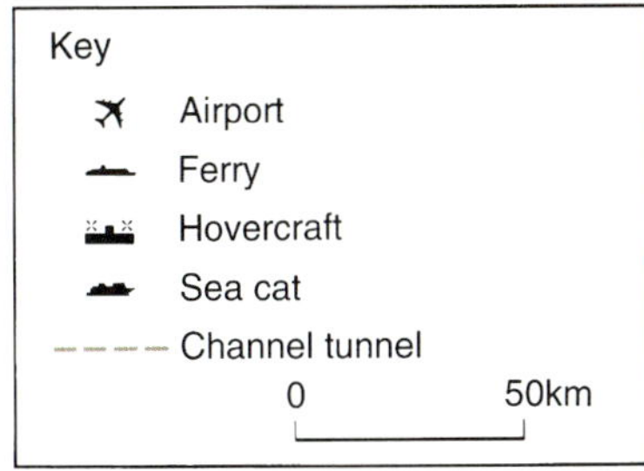
Key
Airport
Ferry
Hovercraft
Sea cat
Channel tunnel
0
50km

N
North Sea
5 scheduled airlines
8 scheduled airlines
Luton
Stansted
Felixstowe
Harwich
Zeebrugge 5–7hrs
Goteborg 24hrs
Esjberg 19hrs
Hamburg 18½hrs
Hook of Holland 6–8hrs
London City
London
56 scheduled airlines
Heathrow
Tilbury
Sheerness
Ramsgate
Ostend 4hrs
5 scheduled airlines
34 scheduled airlines
Gatwick
Dover
Folkestone
2½hrs
1¾hrs
1½hrs
Dunkirk
Calais
Southampton
Newhaven
40mins
Boulogne
Portsmouth
Channel tunnel
Cherbourg 6hrs
Le Havre 7hrs
Caen 7hrs
Cherbourg 7 hrs
St Malo 10hrs
Santander 32hrs
Dieppe 4 hrs
English Channel

Heathrow is the world's busiest international airport. There are flights to and from 220 destinations world-wide. 40 million travellers use the airport each year.

Tasks

5 List the airports in order. Put the busiest airport first.

6 Why do you think London needs so many airports?

7 List the 3 busiest ferry ports.

8 Why do you think a rail link was made rather than a road through the tunnel?

9 Copy and complete the chart.

To	From	Time journey takes
Dieppe		
		19 hours
	Southampton	
Ostend		
	Portsmouth	10 hours
Goteborg		

10 Use an atlas to find the countries in which each destination port is located.

11 Look at this picture of a container ship. Why have new docks been built at Tilbury at the mouth of the Thames?

The Euro tunnel is another way of crossing to the continent. It provides a fast rail link for goods, vehicles and passengers.

LONDON

Living in London

People live in different parts of the city but all can experience the special nature of a capital.

4
3
2
1
2
3
4

This shows how a city grows outwards from its old centre.

Tasks

1 Which zone is
a) the oldest part of the city?
b) the newest part of the city?
c) the most densely populated?

2 Look at the photographs below. In which zone might you find each?

3 Compare the four photographs with your own locality. Which are similar to buildings in your area?

Key

ZONES

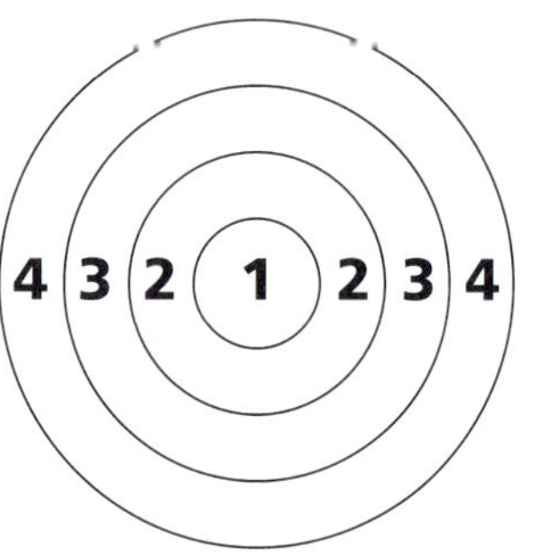
4 3 2 1 2 3 4

1 Old historical city centre, now business, main shopping and entertainment area.

2 Older terraced housing, inner city high rise flats.

3 Inner suburbs – semi detached, larger housing.

4 Outer suburbs – newer houses, new towns, old villages.

A
THEATRE ROYAL DRURY LANE
Miss Saigon

B

C

D

Images of inner London.

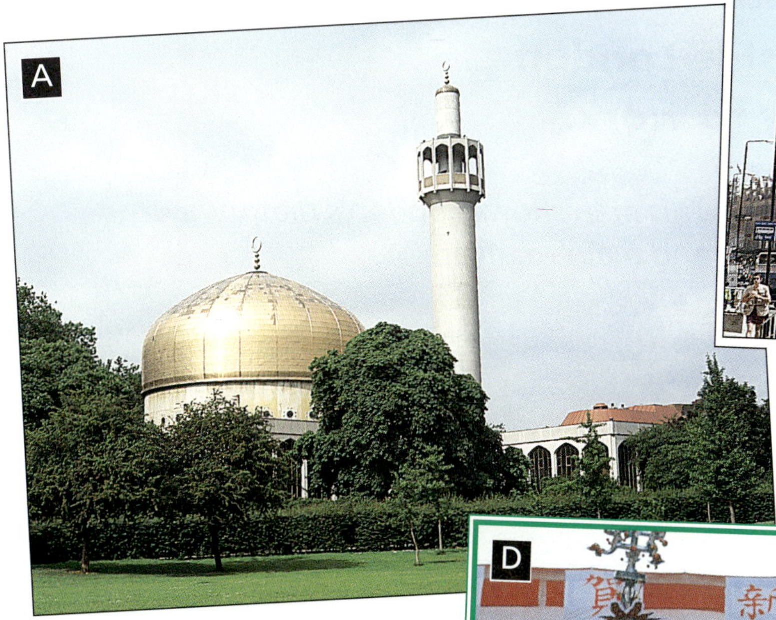

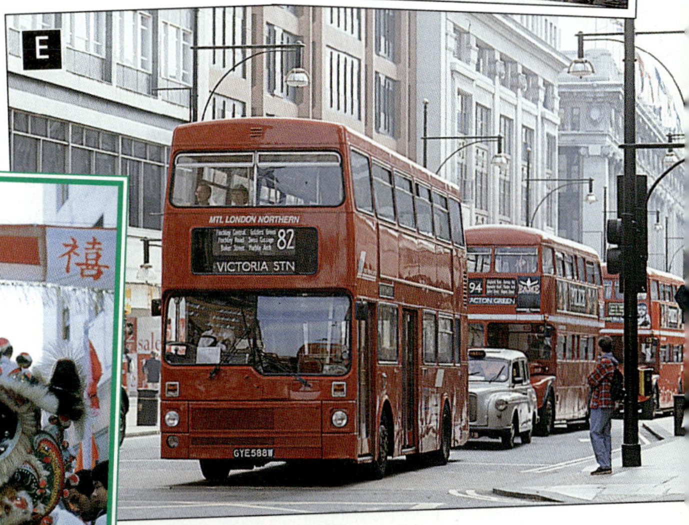

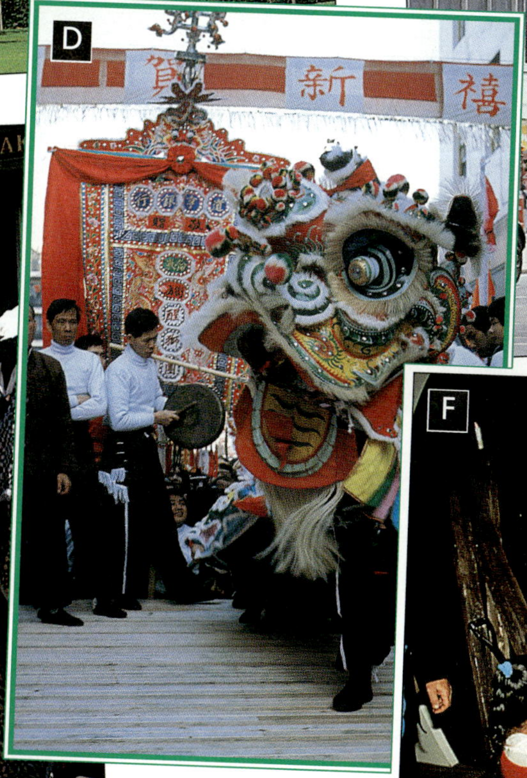

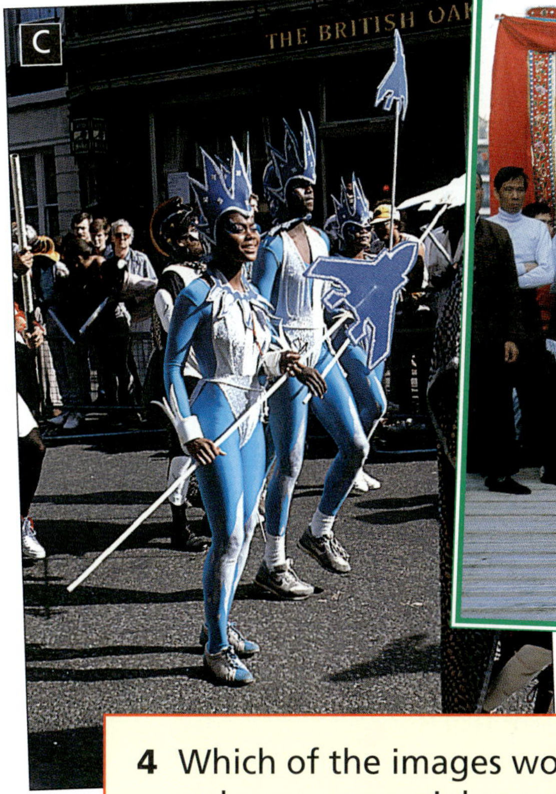

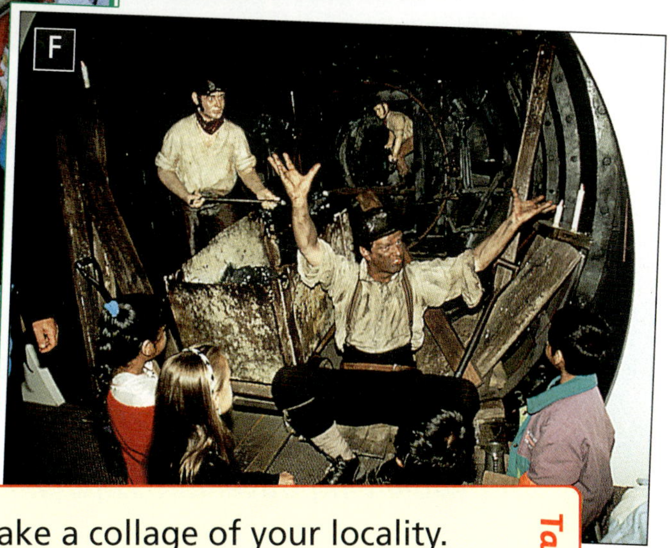

A

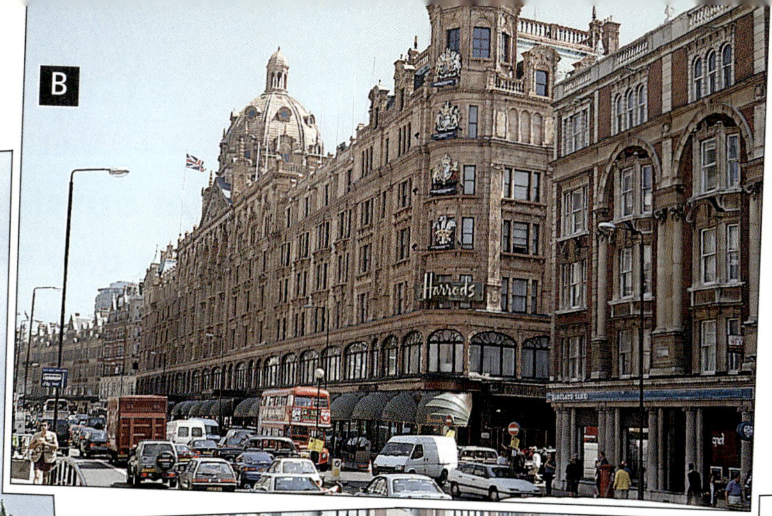

B

E

D

C

F

Tasks

4 Which of the images would you only see on special occasions?

5 What evidence is there that London is a multicultural city?

6 List the cultures included in the images.

7 Why does London have many 24 hour services? Does your locality have any?

8 Make a collage of your locality. Here is a check-list to help you.

worship
entertainment
shopping
places for school visits
eating out
transport
festivals/events

LONDON

London transport

Many people live outside London and travel in each day to work.

As London became very crowded people moved into the countryside outside the city of London to live. Many of these areas became part of Greater London.

F956 HKM

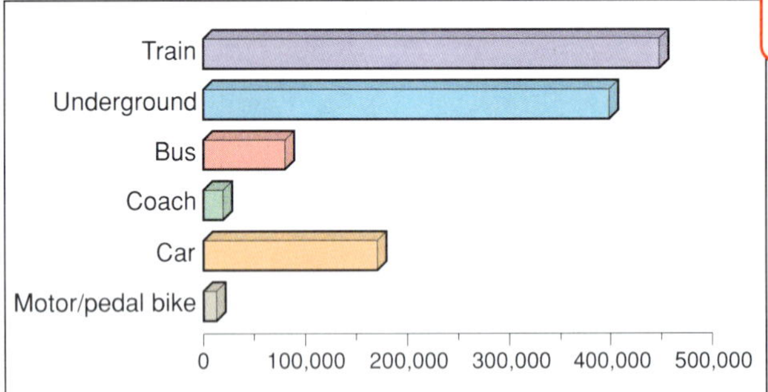
Train
Underground
Bus
Coach
Car
Motor/pedal bike
0
100,000
200,000
300,000
400,000
500,000

This graph shows approximate numbers of people who travel into London each morning, and how they travel.

Fast, frequent, relaxing and refreshing
SWT SHUTTLE

Waterloo Station at rush hour

This map shows London's motorways and main roads.

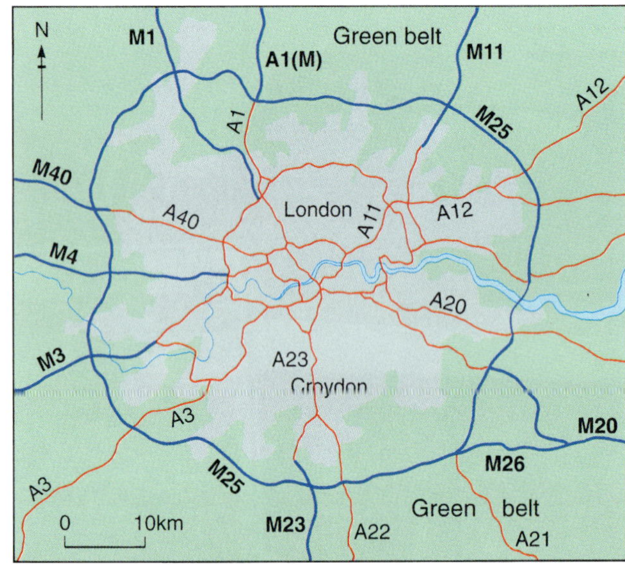
N
M1
A1(M)
Green belt
M11
A12
M25
A1
M40
A40
London
A11
A12
M4
A20
M3
A23
Croydon
A3
M20
M26
M25
A3
0
10km
M23
A22
Green belt
A21

Tasks

Look at the photographs and map on this page.

1. Why do you think travelling by train is the most popular form of transport?
2. Give two reasons why bikes are not used by more people.
3. Which motorways can be used by cars to travel into London from the north?
4. If you lived in Croydon which road would you use to drive into London?
5. The M25 was built around Greater London. Why do you think it was needed?
6. List the advantages and disadvantages of building more roads into or around London.

London Underground

London was so densely populated by the 19th century that no more railways were allowed above the ground. From the 1860s the railways went underground, and the modern 'tube' system was born.

OXFORD CIRCUS
BRIXTON

This map shows the central part of the tube system.

Key to lines
Bakerloo
Central
Circle
District
East London
Hammersmith & City
Jubilee
Metropolitan
Northern
Piccadilly
Victoria
Docklands Light Railway
British Rail
Peak hours only
Restricted service
Peak hours and Sunday mornings
Under construction
UNDERGROUND
Amersham
Chesham
Uxbridge
Watford
Stanmore
Edgware
High Barnet
Mill Hill East
Cockfosters
Walthamstow Central
Kilburn
Finchley Road & Frognal
West Hampstead
Finchley Road
Swiss Cottage
St. John's Wood
Baker Street
Marylebone
Edgware Road
Paddington
Bayswater
Queensway
Marble Arch
Bond Street
Oxford Circus
Tottenham Court Road
Holborn
Chancery Lane
St. Paul's
Bank
Moorgate
Liverpool Street
Aldgate
Aldgate East
Tower Hill
Monument
London Bridge
Waterloo
Westminster
Embankment
Charing Cross
Leicester Square
Covent Garden
Piccadilly Circus
Green Park
Hyde Park Corner
Knightsbridge
South Kensington
Gloucester Road
Earl's Court
Victoria
St. James's Park
Pimlico
Vauxhall
Brixton
Morden
Elephant & Castle
Kennington
Lambeth North
Southwark
Borough
Euston
Euston Square
King's Cross St. Pancras
Warren Street
Goodge Street
Russell Square
Great Portland Street
Regent's Park
Camden Town
Chalk Farm
Kentish Town
Mornington Crescent
Angel
Farringdon
Barbican
Old Street
Highbury & Islington
Ealing Broadway
Ealing Common
Acton Town
Hammersmith
Richmond
Kew Gardens
Gunnersbury
Wimbledon
Heathrow Terminals 1, 2, 3
Heathrow Terminal 4
Hounslow Central
Hounslow West
Hatton Cross
Upminster
Whitechapel
Tower Gateway
Wapping
Rotherhithe
New Cross
New Cross Gate
Bermondsey
River Thames
Interchange stations
Connections with British Rail
Connections with British Rail within walking distance
Airport interchange
Closed Sundays
Closed Saturdays and Sundays
Mornington Crescent closed for rebuilding
For opening times see poster journey planners
Certain stations are closed during public holidays
© London Regional Transport
Diary 1F 4 94

Tasks

Each line has a name and a colour. To travel from Oxford Circus to Bond Street you would take the red route (Central line).

7 Give reasons why an underground system is important for a large city.

8 Look at the graph. How many people travel into London by tube each day?

9 List the advantages and disadvantages of travelling across London by tube, bus, taxi or car.

10 You arrive in London by train at Euston Station. Describe which lines you would use, and where you would change trains to visit the following places:

Place to visit	Nearest tube station
The Prince of Wales Theatre	Leicester Square
The Tower of London	Tower Hill
Shops on Oxford Street	Oxford Circus
Harrod's store	South Kensington

11 List the tube stations you would pass through for each journey.

LONDON

London: a tourist city

Tourists need maps to help them find the places they wish to visit.

Tasks

1 In which grid squares do you find these railway stations

a) Euston b) Victoria
c) St Pancras d) Charing Cross
e) Waterloo e) City Thameslink?

2 List the grid squares through which the River Thames flows.

3 List the places you could visit in

a) (21, 47) b) (22, 48)
c) (20, 46) d) (21, 48)

A

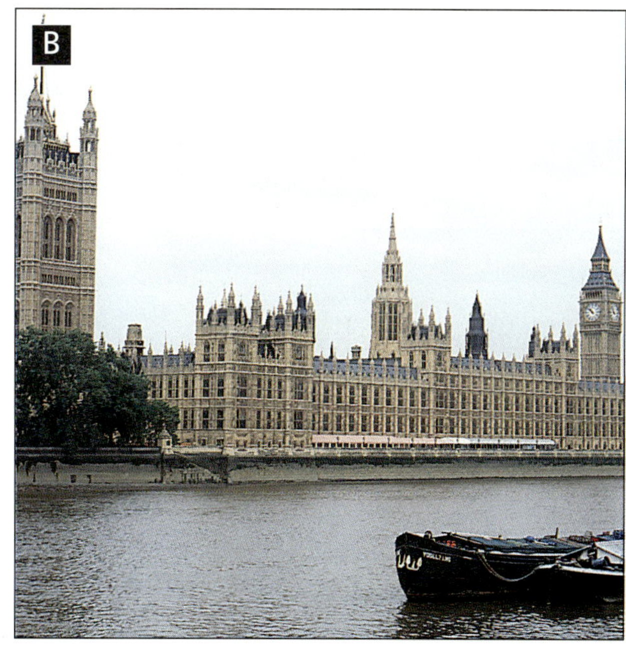
B

C
See
and
be
seen
581
WOODFORD
NAPIER ARMS
via ESSEX ROAD
EXV 253

D

Tasks

4 Copy and complete the chart.

Feature	Photo	Grid square	Activity which takes place there
London Bridge			
Buckingham Palace			
Houses of Parliament			
London Transport Museum			

Tasks

5 Many visitors see the city from the River Thames. The boat sails from London Bridge to Westminster Bridge. List in order the places of interest the boat passes and their grid squares.

6 Plan a day for yourself in London.

a) Choose six places to visit.

b) Say where you would go and why.

THE RHINE

The Rhine: gateway to Europe

The Rhine is one of Europe's most important rivers.

The River Rhine is used for drinking, trade, waste disposal, industry and leisure. It is one of the world's most important inland waterways. It carries ships and barges loaded with cargoes which would otherwise be transported by road or rail. The use of water is a cheap form of transport.

The captains and crew of the barges spend their working lives on the Rhine. Some have their families with them as they are away from home for long periods. Most carry a car to use when the barge is moored.

Tasks

1 In which country is the source of the River Rhine?

2 From which mountain range does it flow?

3 Through which lake does it flow?

4 In which sea is the mouth of the Rhine?

5 Name, in order, the countries the Rhine passes through from source to mouth.

6 In which direction does it flow?

Cargo carried from Rotterdam

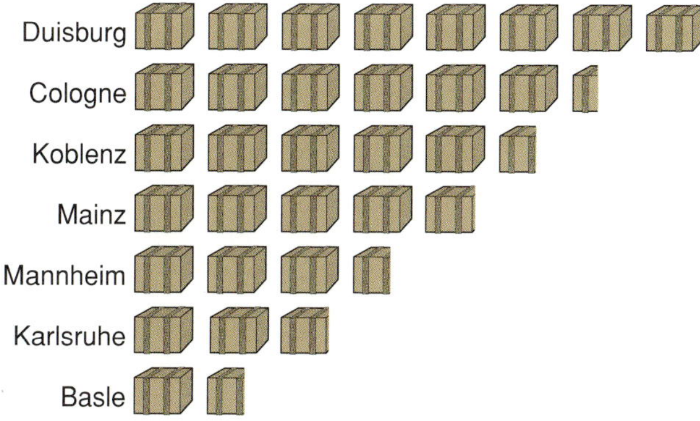
Duisburg
Cologne
Koblenz
Mainz
Mannheim
Karlsruhe
Basle
= 10 million tonnes

The river becomes narrower and shallower the further it is from Rotterdam. Only smaller barges can reach Basle.

Size limit of boats	
size	**can reach**
ocean going	Rotterdam
7000 tonnes	Duisberg
6000 tonnes	Mannheim
2500 tonnes	Strasbourg
2000 tonnes	Basle

Tasks

7 To which city is the most cargo carried from Rotterdam?

8 Why is less cargo carried to Basle than to Cologne?

9 Complete a captain's journey log from Rotterdam to Basle. You travel 120km a day.

port	distance	time
Rotterdam		
Duisberg		
Koblenz		
Mannheim		
Strasbourg		
Basle		

The Rhine network

People have used rivers for transport since earliest times.

N
Norway
Oslo
Stockholm
Sweden
Baltic Sea
North Sea
Denmark
Copenhagen
Eire
United Kingdom
R. Thames
Kiel
Kiel Canal
Bremerhaven
Hamburg
Küsten Canal
Elbe Lateral Canal
Bremen
Netherlands
Mittelland Canal
Hannover
Poland
Rotterdam
R. Ems
Dortmund-Ems Canal
Duisburg
Dortmund
R. Weser
R. Elbe
Antwerp
Albert Canal
Cologne
Germany
Dunkirk-Valenciennes Canal
Belgium
Koblenz
Le Havre
Frankfurt
R. Main
Czech Republic
Luxembourg
R. Moselle
Mainz
R. Seine
Paris
Mannheim
Main-Danube Canal
Karlsruhe
R. Marne
Strasbourg
Slovakia
R. Loire
Est Canal
R. Rhine
R. Danube
Marne-Saône Canal
Basle
Austria
Bay of Biscay
Rhône-Rhine Canal
Switzerland
Hungary
France
to Black Sea
R. Saône
Slovenia
Croatia
Bordeaux
R. Garonne
R. Po
Bosnia-Herzegovina
Garonne Lateral Canal
R. Rhône
Midi canal
Marseille
Italy
Spain
Adriatic Sea
Key
Canals
Rivers
0
250
500km
Mediterranean Sea

Where no natural river flows an artificial river can be built. This is called a 'canal'. Canals have existed since ancient times. They provide short cuts along which cargoes can be carried saving time and money.

The Rhine and its tributaries are linked by canals to other major European rivers. The most recent canal is the Main-Danube Canal which enables barges up to 1350 tonnes to travel from the North Sea to the Black Sea. The photo above shows it being built.

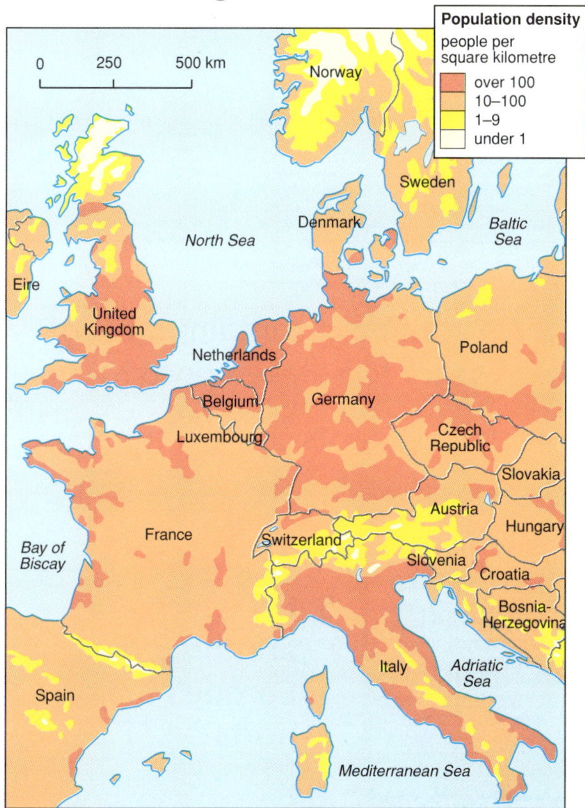

Population density
people per square kilometre
over 100
10–100
1–9
under 1
0
250
500 km
Norway
Sweden
Denmark
Baltic Sea
North Sea
Eire
United Kingdom
Netherlands
Poland
Belgium
Germany
Luxembourg
Czech Republic
Slovakia
Austria
Hungary
France
Switzerland
Slovenia
Croatia
Bay of Biscay
Bosnia-Herzegovina
Italy
Adriatic Sea
Spain
Mediterranean Sea

Tasks

Find the Kiel Canal on the map opposite.

1 Which two seas does it connect?

2 What is the alternative water route between Bremerhaven and Kiel?

3 Use an atlas. Which two seas are connected by

a) The Suez Canal
b) The Panama Canal?

4 Imagine neither canal has been built. Use an atlas to describe alternative routes.

5 Copy and complete the chart to show routes by waterway from Rotterdam.

To	Route
Baltic Sea	
Mediterranean Sea	
Black Sea	

6 Which city stands on the confluence of the Rhine and Moselle?

7 Use tracing paper and the scale bar on the population map. Draw and cut out a circle with a radius of 500 km. Put the centre of your circle on Rotterdam.

8 List the countries wholly or partly covered by the circle.

9 What do you notice about the number of people living in a 500km radius of Rotterdam compared to the rest of the map?

10 Explain why this is important to factory owners and business people.

THE RHINE

Rotterdam: the world's busiest cargo port

Rotterdam has excellent dock facilities and water, rail, and road links with the whole of Europe.

Traders from all around the world send their goods to Rotterdam. These are then redirected to their destinations. European exporters send their goods to Rotterdam for loading onto ocean going ships to the rest of the world.

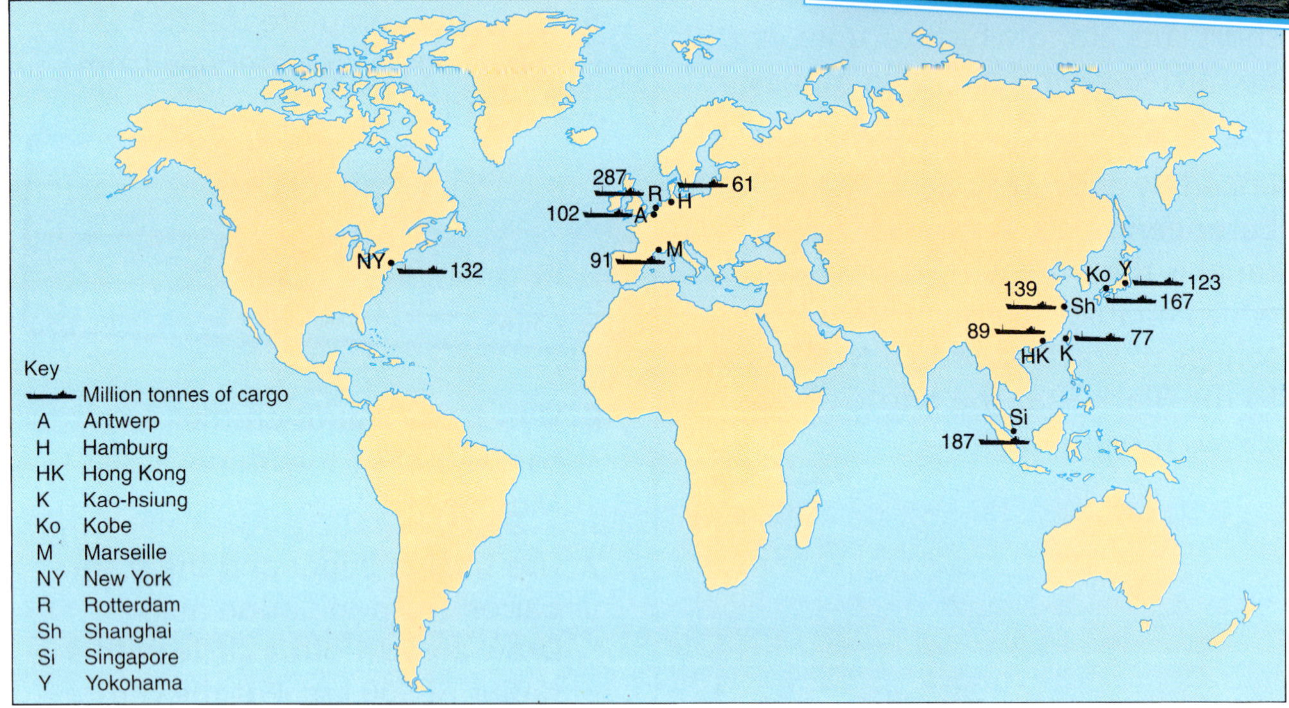
287
R
H
61
102
A
NY
132
91
M
139
Ko
Y
123
Sh
167
89
77
HK
K
Si
187
Key
Million tonnes of cargo
A Antwerp
H Hamburg
HK Hong Kong
K Kao-hsiung
Ko Kobe
M Marseille
NY New York
R Rotterdam
Sh Shanghai
Si Singapore
Y Yokohama

Tasks

The map shows the eleven busiest ports in the world. Use an atlas.

1 Copy and complete the chart. List the ports starting with the busiest.

port	cargo in tonnes	country	continent
Rotterdam	287 million	Netherlands	Europe

2 Which continent contains most of the world's top eleven ports?

3 Which continents contain none?

4 Which country has more than one in the list?

5 On which sea are three of Europe's major ports?

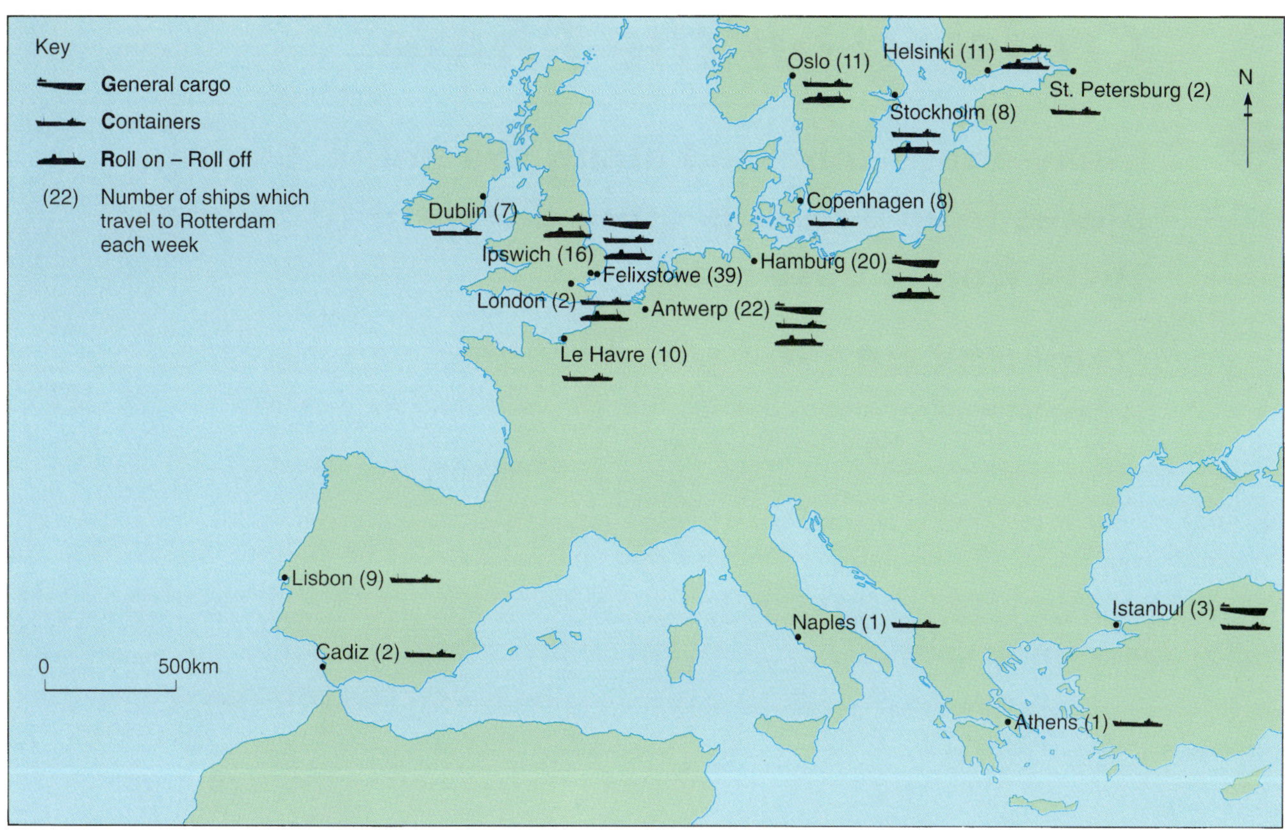
Key
General cargo
Containers
Roll on – Roll off
(22) Number of ships which travel to Rotterdam each week
Oslo (11)
Helsinki (11)
St. Petersburg (2)
N
Stockholm (8)
Copenhagen (8)
Dublin (7)
Ipswich (16)
Hamburg (20)
Felixstowe (39)
London (2)
Antwerp (22)
Le Havre (10)
Lisbon (9)
Naples (1)
Istanbul (3)
Cadiz (2)
0
500km
Athens (1)

The map above shows the European ports which Rotterdam trades with every week.

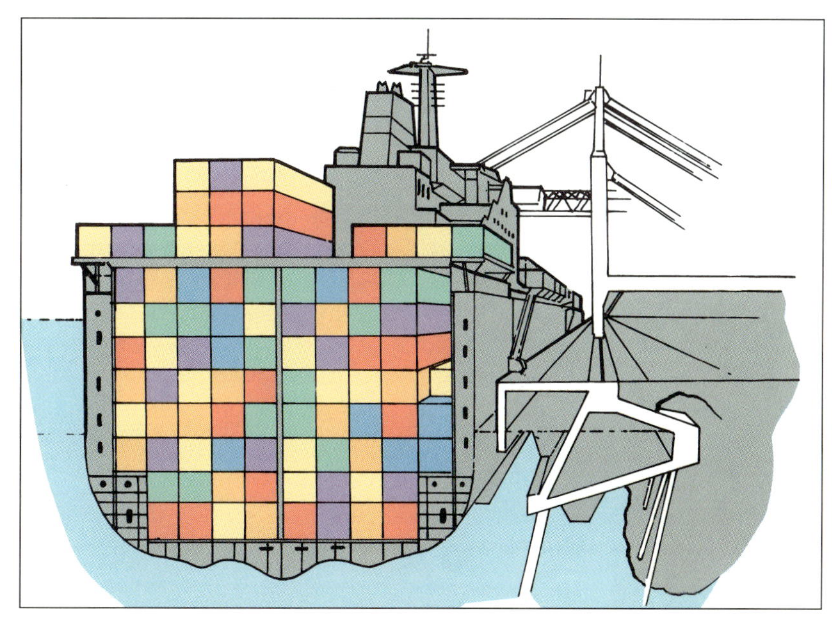

Containers hold a wide variety of goods. They can be unloaded at a port for further transportation or the whole container placed on a train or truck for its final destination.

Tasks

6 Copy and complete the chart. List the European ports with which Rotterdam trades starting with the highest number of ships per week. Tick the appropriate cargo boxes.

port	ships per week	country	G	C	R
Felixstowe	39	UK			

7 How many UK ports trade with Rotterdam?

8 On which coast are they? Can you explain this pattern?

9 Why do Athens, Naples and Istanbul have less trade with Rotterdam than Antwerp, Hamburg and Helsinki?

Cruising on the Rhine

Many cruise ships sail along the Rhine. Seeing places from a river is quite different to seeing them from a busy road.

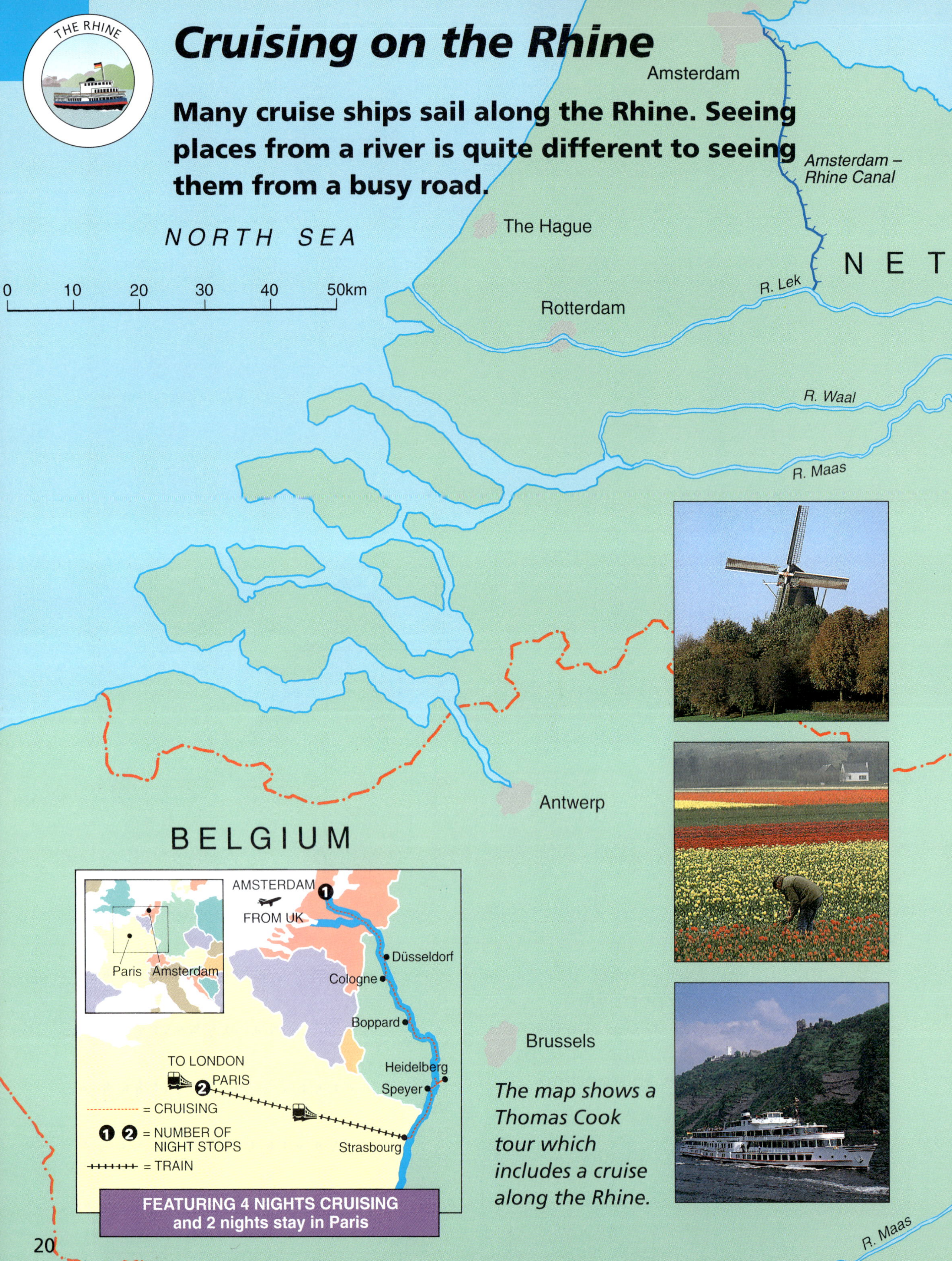
THE RHINE
Amsterdam
Amsterdam – Rhine Canal
The Hague
NORTH SEA
N E T
0 10 20 30 40 50km
R. Lek
Rotterdam
R. Waal
R. Maas
Antwerp
BELGIUM
Brussels
R. Maas
AMSTERDAM
FROM UK
Paris
Amsterdam
Düsseldorf
Cologne
Boppard
Heidelberg
Speyer
TO LONDON
PARIS
Strasbourg
= CRUISING
= NUMBER OF NIGHT STOPS
= TRAIN
FEATURING 4 NIGHTS CRUISING and 2 nights stay in Paris

The map shows a Thomas Cook tour which includes a cruise along the Rhine.

R L A N D S
R. Rhine
R. Maas
Düsseldorf
GERMANY
N

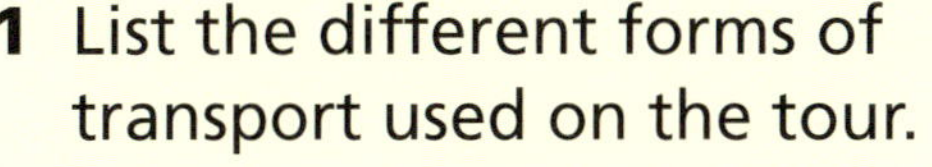

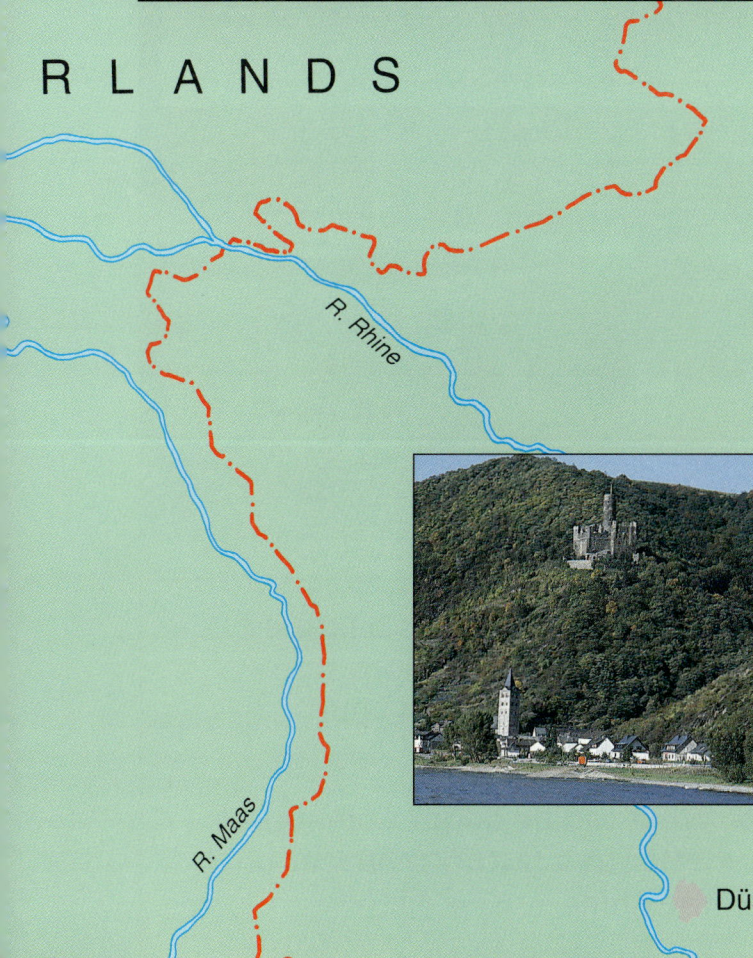

ROMANTIC RHINE AND PARIS
ITINERARY

Day 1	**Fly from London to Amsterdam.** Coach transfer to hotel.
Day 2	**Visit Amsterdam.** Join the cruiser in the evening.
Day 3	**Cruise from Amsterdam to Dusseldorf.** Begin along the Rhine-Amsterdam Canal to join the Rhine into Germany. See the famous Ruhr region. Dock overnight.
Day 4	**Dusseldorf to Cologne to Boppard.** Visit Cologne city centre in the morning. View the Cathedral. Cruise along the romantic Rhine seeing castles, sleepy villages and vineyards. Dock at Boppard.
Day 5	**Boppard to Heidelberg to Speyer.** Cruise past the Lorelei Rock and the wine region. Visit romantic Heidelberg. Dock at Speyer.
Day 6	**Speyer to Strasbourg to Paris.** Cruise to Strasbourg, transfer to a train. Travel by train to Paris.
Day 7	**Sight seeing in Paris.**
Day 8	**Travel from Paris through the tunnel by train to London.**

Tasks

1 List the different forms of transport used on the tour.

2 Which countries do holiday makers pass through on this tour?

3 List the places where the cruiser docks overnight.

4 Look at the list of special interests people might have. Which would be the best day or days for them?

Interest	Best day/s
religion	
eating Dutch cheese	
city centre shopping	
buying German wine	
photographing historic sites	

5 How many of the eight days are actually spent cruising?

6 How far do tourists from London travel altogether?

7 Is the Rhine shown at the correct scale on the tour map? If not, why not?

THE RHINE

The Rhine: Pollution

Human beings use rivers to carry away waste. The Rhine has been called 'Europe's largest sewer'.

As the Rhine flows north it is contaminated with oil, lead, mercury, arsenic, potash, cadmium and other chemicals. Heat from power stations warms the water and reduces its oxygen. Chemicals from the land feed the river, bacteria increases and oxygen is used up. Fish and other river life cannot survive. Major efforts are now being made to clean up the Rhine.

30 tonnes of mercury and other chemicals were washed into the Rhine from the Sandoz chemical plant, near Basle, killing millions of fish.

Tasks

1. Why is so much industry located along the Rhine?
2. Why are there so many power stations?
3. List the cities where the river is at risk from
   a) chemicals
   b) oil
   c) increased heating.
4. Should the factories be closed and the power stations stop production? Explain your answer.
5. What can be done? Compose a letter to a factory manager on the Rhine.
6. What can governments do?

The salmon's fight for survival.

Fish, including the salmon live in the sea but must swim up the river to breed. The pollution led to many species of fish disappearing from the Rhine.

Sea
Chemicals
Heat
Lack of oxygen
Metals

N
NETHERLANDS
North Sea
Rotterdam
R. Lippe
Duisburg
R. Ruhr
Düsseldorf
Cologne
GERMANY
BELGIUM
R. Maas
Koblenz
R. Main
Mainz
LUXEMBOURG
R. Mosel
Biblis
Mannheim
Karlsruhe
FRANCE
R. Rhine
R. Neckar
Fessenhein
Basle
Lake Constance
SWITZERLAND
Key
Chemical industry
Oil refinery
Nuclear power station
Coal power station
Other industries
0
100km

KENYA

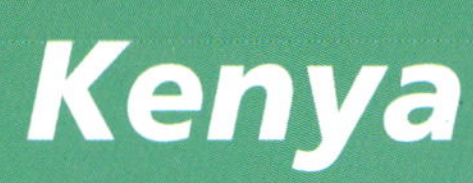
Kenya

Kenya

Kenya is a country in East Africa.

AFRICA
Kenya

Here is a map showing the location of Kenya.

The capital city is Nairobi which is in the south west part of the country, on the edge of the Kenyan Highlands.

A
N
SUDAN
ETHIOPIA
UGANDA
KENYA
SOMALIA
Nairobi
TANZANIA
Mombasa
Indian Ocean
0
200km

B
N
SUDAN
ETHIOPIA
Lake Turkana
UGANDA
KENYA
SOMALIA
Rift Valley
Aberdare Mountains
0°
Equator
Lake Victoria
Mt. Kenya 5200m
Nairobi
R. Tana
Coastal Plain
R. Athi
TANZANIA
Mombasa
Indian Ocean
0
200km

Tasks

Look at maps A and B.

1 Copy and complete this chart showing the countries bordering Kenya.

Direction	**Name of country**
North	
East	
West	
North West	
South West	

2 Which ocean lies to the South East of Kenya?

3 What is the name of the main town on the coastal plain of Kenya?

4 Which important line of latitude runs through Kenya?

5 What is the height of Mount Kenya?

6 Use an atlas to find out the name and height of the famous mountain which is close to the border of Kenya and Tanzania.

Population distribution

- *20% of Kenya's population live in towns and cities such as Nairobi and Mombasa.*
- *The remaining 80% of the population live in rural areas.*

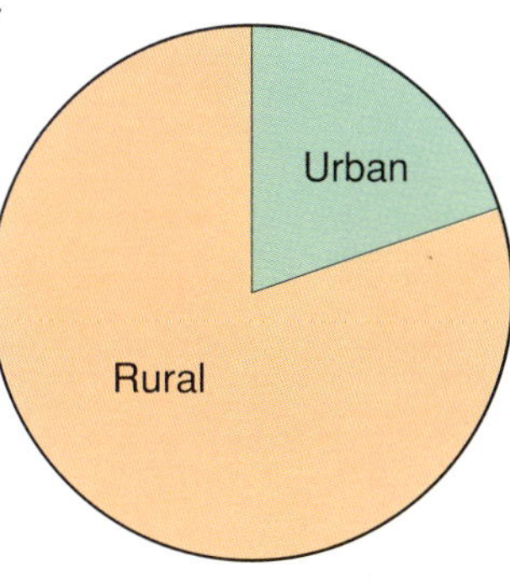

Urban
Rural

Climatic regions

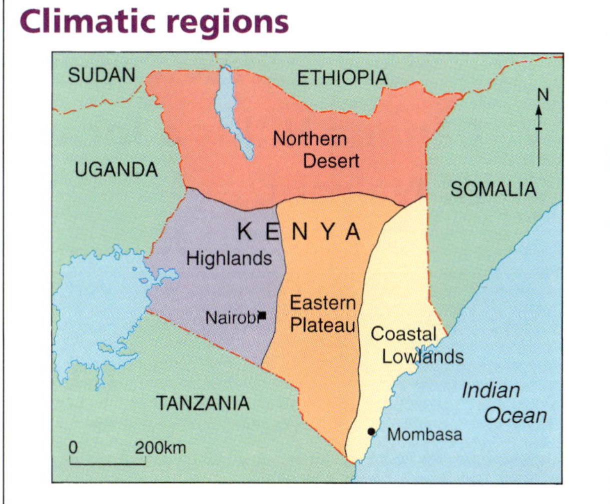

SUDAN
ETHIOPIA
N
UGANDA
Northern Desert
SOMALIA
KENYA
Highlands
Nairobi
Eastern Plateau
Coastal Lowlands
TANZANIA
Indian Ocean
Mombasa
0
200km

Population change

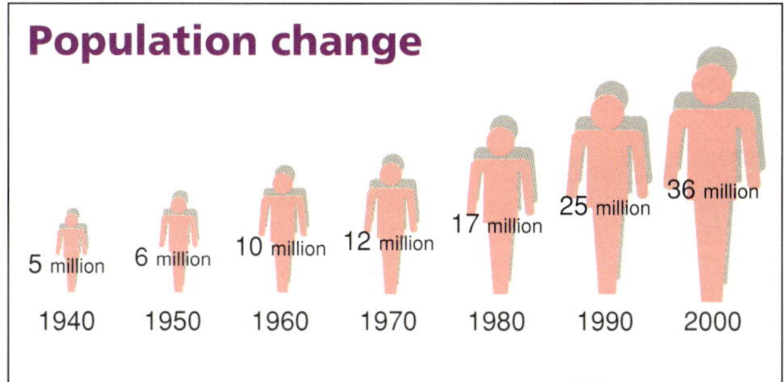

5 million
6 million
10 million
12 million
17 million
25 million
36 million
1940
1950
1960
1970
1980
1990
2000

Age structure

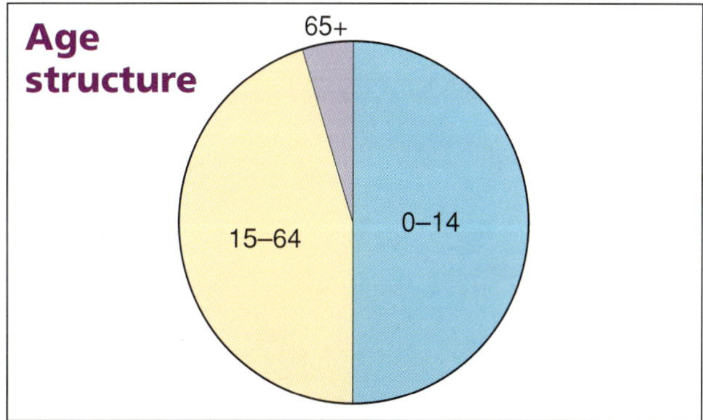

65+
15–64
0–14

Fact File – Nairobi

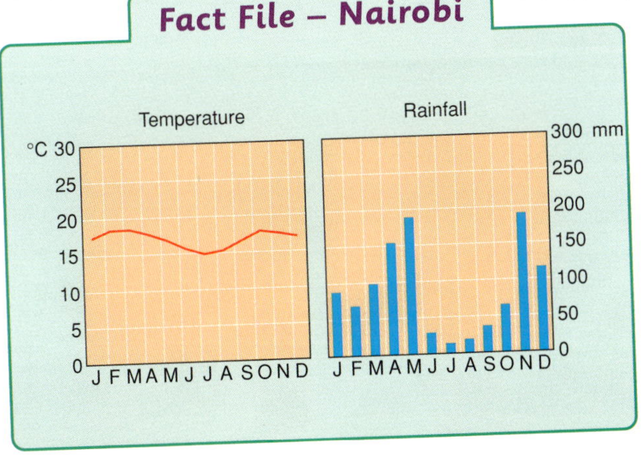

Temperature
Rainfall
°C 30
25
20
15
10
5
0
J F M A M J J A S O N D
300 mm
250
200
150
100
50
0

Fact File – Mombasa

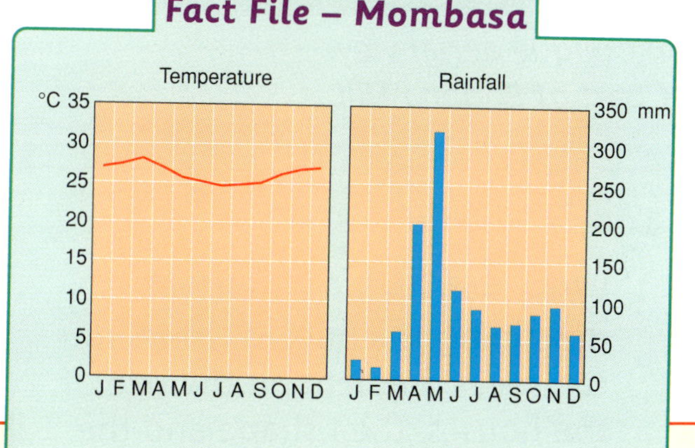

Temperature
Rainfall
°C 35
30
25
20
15
10
5
0
J F M A M J J A S O N D
350 mm
300
250
200
150
100
50
0

Tasks

7 What are the four main climatic regions of Kenya?

8 In which region is Nairobi and in which region is Mombasa?

9 Which city receives the most rainfall?

10 How much annual rainfall do each of the two cities receive?

11 Which city experiences the lower temperatures? Explain why you think this is so.

12 What has happened to the population of Kenya since 1940?

13 Describe the age structure of the population of Kenya.

14 Young children do not work for a living but they have many needs. List three.

15 What problems does the government have with so many children?

KENYA

Banana Hill

Banana Hill is a locality 20km north of the city of Nairobi.

An oblique aerial view of part of Banana Hill.

Banana Hill is a suburb of Nairobi. About 10,000 people live in Banana Hill.

SUDAN
ETHIOPIA
N
UGANDA
KENYA
SOMALIA
Banana Hill
Nairobi
TANZANIA
Mombasa
Indian Ocean
0
200km

Tasks

Look at the houses in Banana Hill.

1 Write two or three sentences describing the houses which you can see. Comment on the size of the houses, their shape and the building materials used.

2 Compare this locality with your own local area. Make a list of the similarities and differences.

Look at the photograph of the city centre of Nairobi.

3 How is it different from Banana Hill?

4 How do the price of houses in Nairobi compare to the price of houses in Banana Hill?

5 Give three reasons why you think some people choose to live in Banana Hill rather than in Nairobi.

Price of a typical house in:	Kenyan Shillings
Nairobi	1,500,000
Banana Hill	800,000

Here are some photographs of Banana Hill.

A

School

B

Market

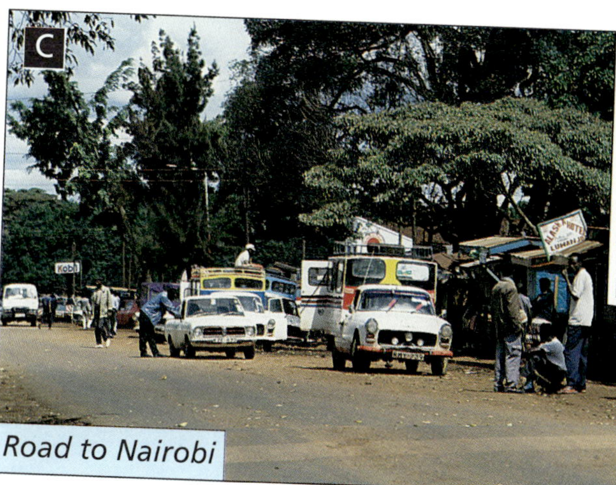
C

Road to Nairobi

D

Catholic church

Service	Grid Ref.	Photo No.
School		
Catholic Church		
Market		
Road to Nairobi		

Here is a map of Banana Hill showing the location of the main services available.

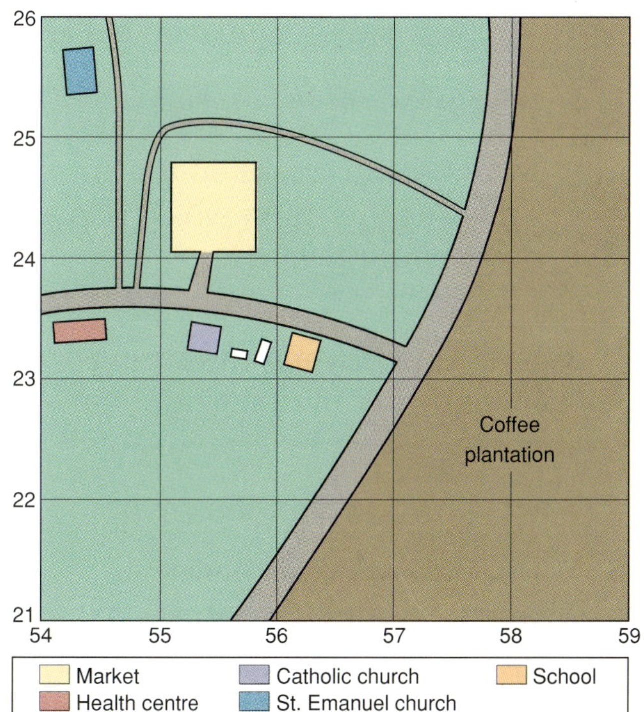
26
25
24
23
22
21
54
55
56
57
58
59
Coffee plantation
Market
Catholic church
School
Health centre
St. Emanuel church

Tasks

6 Copy and complete this table.

7 Make a list of the services in your local area.

8 How is the main road to Nairobi different to a main road in your local area?

9 Which building is different from the rest of the buildings in the locality and why?

10 Choose the photograph of either the school or the market. What can you see in the photograph? How is it the same and/or different to the school or market in your locality?

KENYA

The Mwangi family

The Mwangi family lives in Banana Hill.

Leonard and Mary Mwangi and their two youngest children live in Banana Hill. Their house has three bedrooms, a sitting room and a kitchen.

A

This is the Mwangi's house. Elizabeth, their daughter, is hanging out the washing.

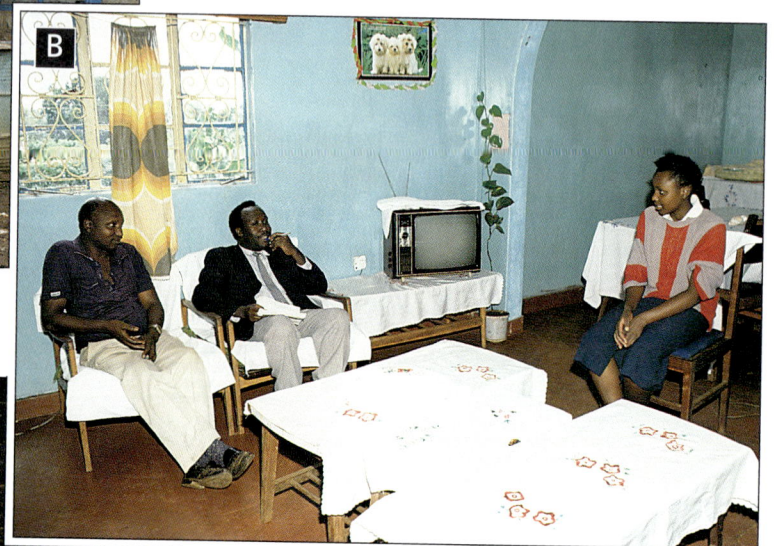

Mr Mwangi is in his sitting room. He is the man on the left.

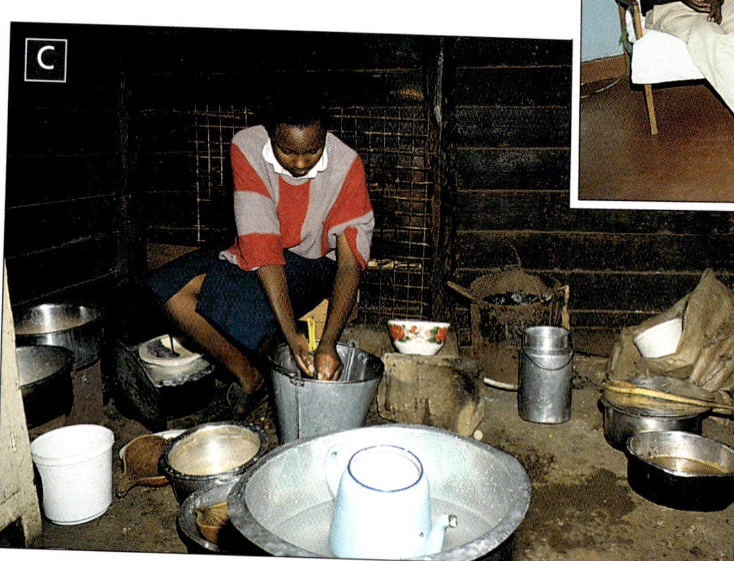
C

Elizabeth is in the kitchen.

Mrs Mwangi works on the family's other farm which is in a neighbouring village.

Tasks

Look at the photographs.

1 What is Elizabeth doing in photograph A?

2 What can you see in Mr Mwangi's sitting room?

3 List the similarities and differences between this sitting room and your own sitting room at home.

4 What can you see in the kitchen?

5 In what ways is this kitchen different to your kitchen at home?

The Mwangi family earns a living in a variety of ways.

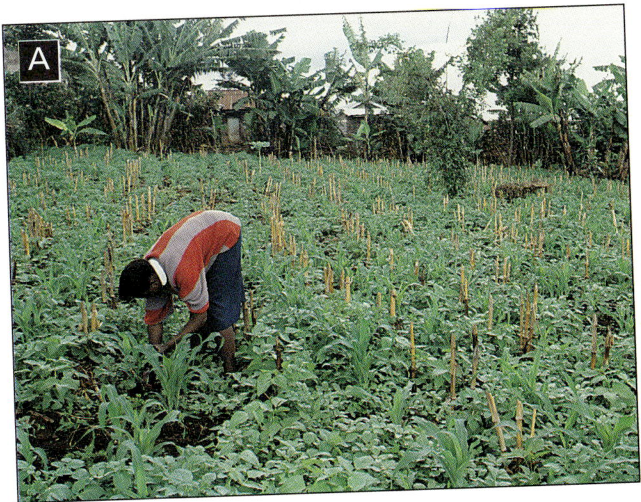
A

The Mwangis grow maize and beans.

B

Mr Mwangi has a kitchenware stall on Karuri market.

C

The Mwangis have three cows which they keep for milk. They sell the milk to the local people.

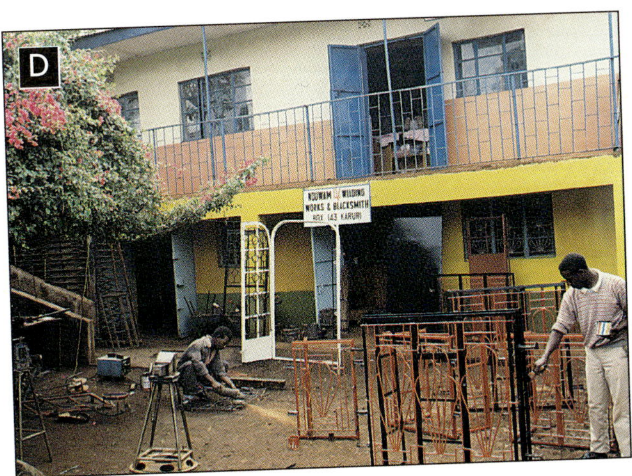
D
WORKS & BLACKSMITH

Mr Mwangi is a blacksmith. He makes steel door frames and steel windows.

Tasks

Use the photographs to help you answer these questions.

6 Who is looking after and weeding Mr Mwangi's maize and bean crops?

7 List three things Mr Mwangi sells on his kitchenware stall in Karuri market. Are they natural products or have they been manufactured?

8 Why are Mr Mwangi's cows not grazing in grassy fields?

9 What breed of cow does Mr Mwangi keep?

10 What are the two men doing in photograph D?

11 Make a list of all the different ways in which the Mwangis earn a living.

12 Why do you think they have so many sources of income?

13 Suggest two ways in which their livelihood could be threatened.

KENYA

Exploiting the forests

Forests provide people with valuable fuel supplies needed for cooking and heating.

Kshs 10/-
Kshs 250/-
CHARCOAL

Mr Mwangi is trying to decide which type of fuel to use.

As the population of Kenya increases large areas of forest are having to be felled to provide wood for firewood and wood to make charcoal. The destruction of large areas of forest often has serious consequences.

Tasks

1 Which two types of fuel is Mr Mwangi able to choose from?

2 Which fuel do you think Mr Mwangi will choose the most often? Why?

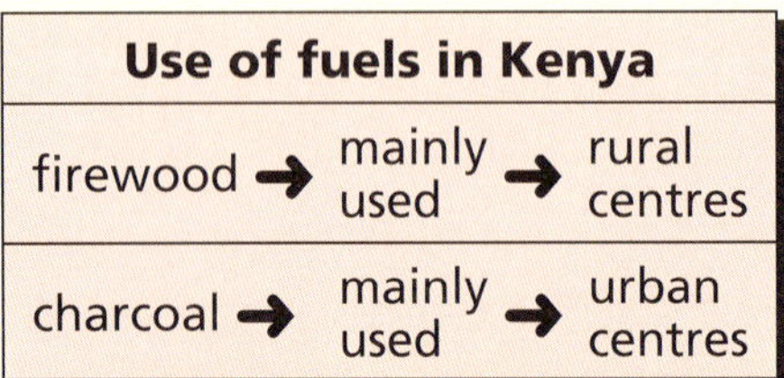

Use of fuels in Kenya				
firewood	➔	mainly used	➔	rural centres
charcoal	➔	mainly used	➔	urban centres

3 Which type of fuel will the people in Nairobi use?

4 Which type of fuel will the people in Banana Hill use?

5 Choose one of the effects in the flow chart.

Design a poster illustrating the effects of the destruction of forests.

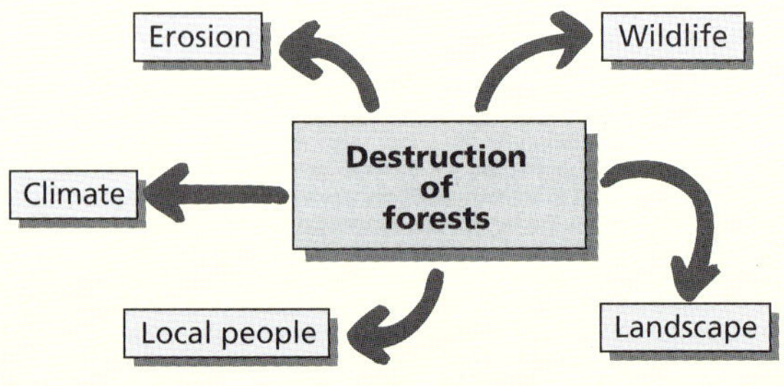
Destruction of forests
Erosion
Wildlife
Climate
Landscape
Local people

Alternative sources of fuel have had to be found.

Timber market
Coffee drying containers
Sawdust
Remains of coffee beans
High quality charcoal

Tasks

6 Which two products are currently being used to form a new type of fuel?

7 List the advantages of these alternative types of fuels.

Energy saving stoves are also being installed.

There are two main types.

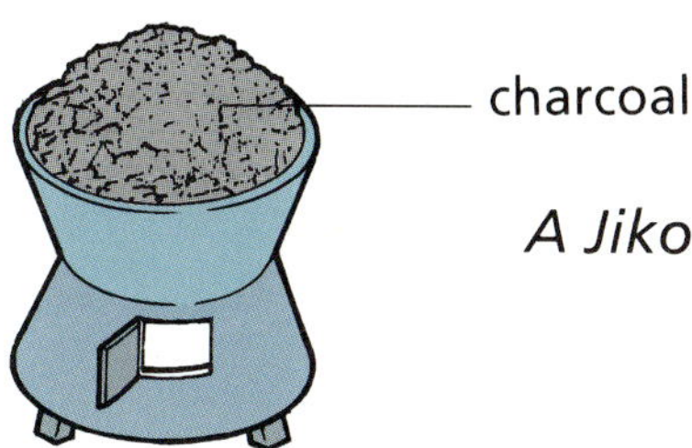
charcoal

A Jiko

They are made of a special clay which retains heat for longer periods of time and so only small amounts of fuels are needed.

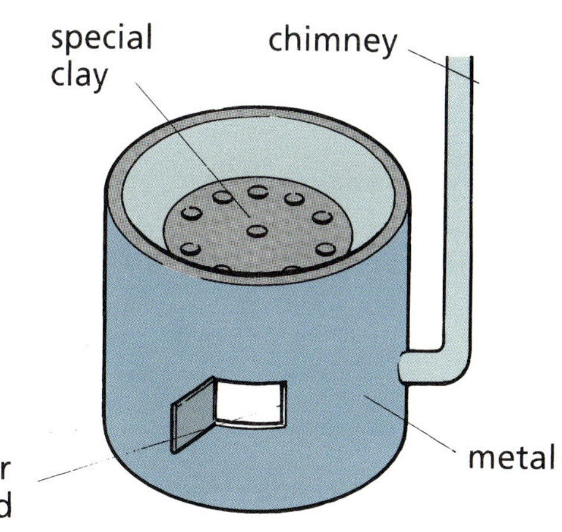
special clay
chimney
space for firewood
metal

A big Jiko with an oven.

Tasks

8 Which type of fuel does each of the jikos use?

9 Which would be the best type of jiko for Mr Mwangi to use in Banana Hill?

10 What special feature have they got which makes them energy saving?

Personal waste

There is more and more waste in the modern world.

Tasks

1 Write a description of what is happening in each picture sequence.

2 Copy and complete the chart.

Contents	Container material	Reason the material is used

3 Waste has an effect on people and a cost in money. For each picture sequence write how people are affected and the possible costs, (for example, hospital treatment).

4 Draw a picture sequence for each of the three issues showing how things could be improved.

Who is responsible?

I only provide the container. Don't blame me if it's thrown away.

It's not my fault. The litter bins are always full.

I work for the council but what can I do? The containers are so big and light we would need litter bins on every lamp-post and workers to empty them every two hours.

Tasks

5 Write what each person could do to improve matters.

6 Investigate your nearest fast food take away store.
a) Is there litter nearby?
b) Is it food packaging?
c) Are there litter bins?
d) Who provides them?
e) Are they full?
f) How could things be improved?

3d DEPOSIT ON bottle

Tasks

7 Describe how each past event reduced waste.

8 Which are still possible today?

9 Draw three pictures showing what happens today.

PEOPLE AND THE ENVIRONMENT

Nuclear waste

Some types of waste are more dangerous than others.

N
Key
Nuclear power stations
Motorways
Railways
Dounreay
Torness
Glasgow
Edinburgh
Hunterston B
Chapelcross
CUMBRIA
Lake District
Newcastle
Hartlepool
Belfast
Calder Hall
Sellafield
Heysham 1, 2
Leeds
Dublin
Wylfa
Liverpool
Manchester
Trawsfynydd
Birmingham
Sizewell A, B
Bradwell
Cardiff
Oldbury
Bristol
Hinkley Point A, B
Dungeness A, B
Southampton
0
100km

Nuclear waste is very dangerous because it is radio-active. It costs a great deal of money to reprocess or dispose of nuclear waste because of this danger.

At Sellafield in West Cumbria, a company called 'British Nuclear Fuels' reprocesses and stores nuclear waste. A lot of the electricity that we use in Britain is generated using nuclear fuel, and the waste from this fuel has to be recycled at Sellafield or stored while it slowly loses its radio-activity. X-ray technology in hospitals, equipment for checking welding in metals and equipment used in processing food all produce radio-active waste. When radio-active material is received at Sellafield much of it is recycled and used again but that which can't be is treated and then stored in special very thick containers underground.

Tasks

1 Study the map. Decide whether to transport nuclear waste by rail, road or sea from each power station shown in the chart.

Nuclear Power Station	sea	rail	road
Heysham			
Sizewell			
Dungeness			
Hunterston			

2 Describe the danger of transporting nuclear waste;
a) by road,
b) by rail,
c) by sea.

THINK about
Centres of population
Accidents
Plants
Animals
Storms
Recovery

Tasks

3 Describe the location of Sellafield?

4 Why was it not built in the centre of a large city?

5 Why is it on the coast?

6 Why does it have a fence around it?

Sellafield has a large visitors' centre. It advertises free visits.

7 Write three questions someone worried about nuclear waste might ask.

8 What answers would you expect from Sellafield?

PEOPLE AND THE ENVIRONMENT

Electricity

Electricity is essential but it is often wasted.

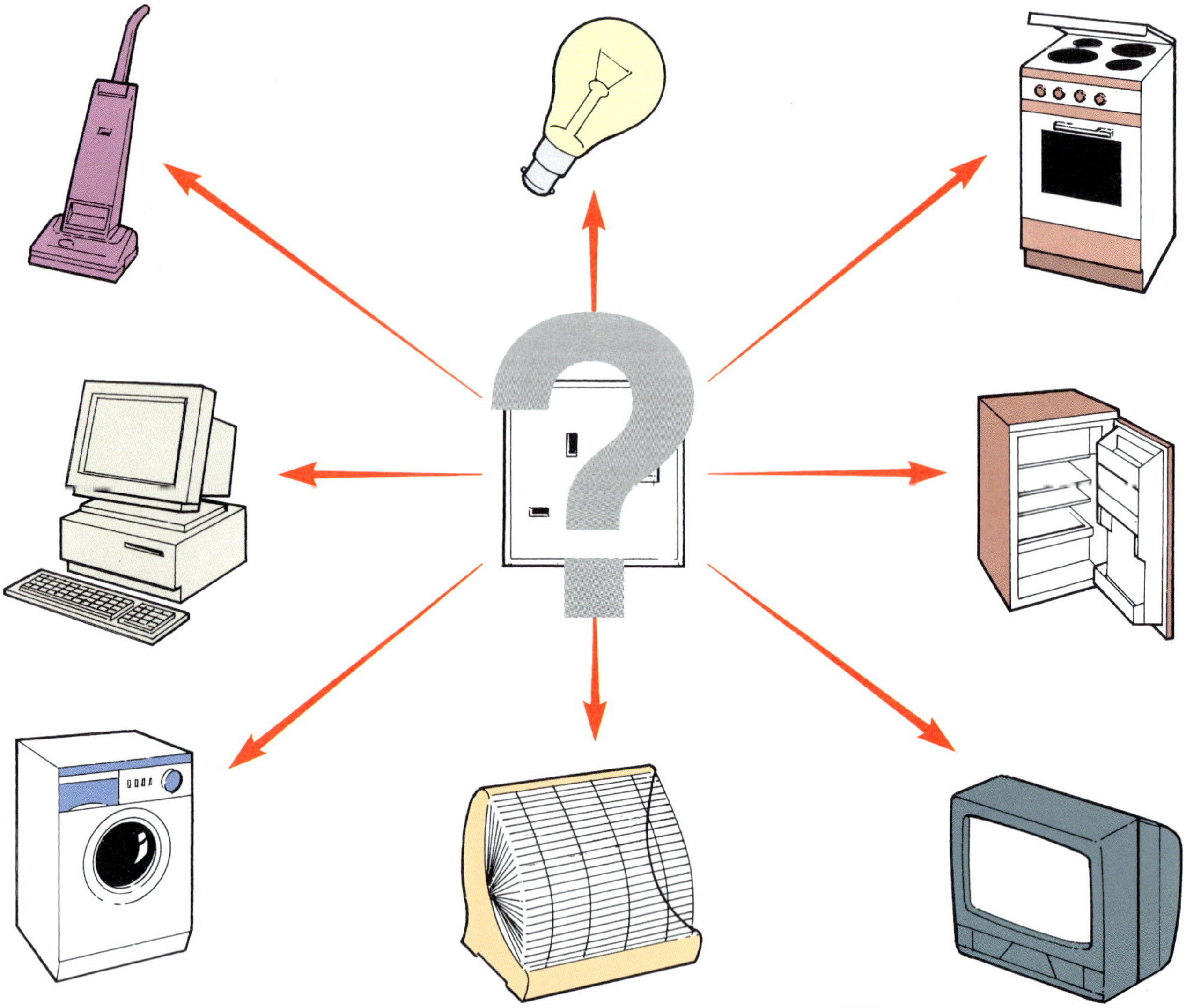

Household item	Purpose	What was used in the past
Electric bulb	To provide light	Gas / candle

Tasks

1 Look at the pictures. Copy and complete the chart.

2 List 10 other electrical items used in your home.

3 Sort the 18 items into:

Essential	Desirable

4 Put the items in your essential list in order of importance.

5 Describe how electricity can be wasted in the use of 5 different items.

6 Design a poster encouraging people to save electricity in a practical way.

Sources of electricity.

Electricity can be produced from a wide variety of sources.

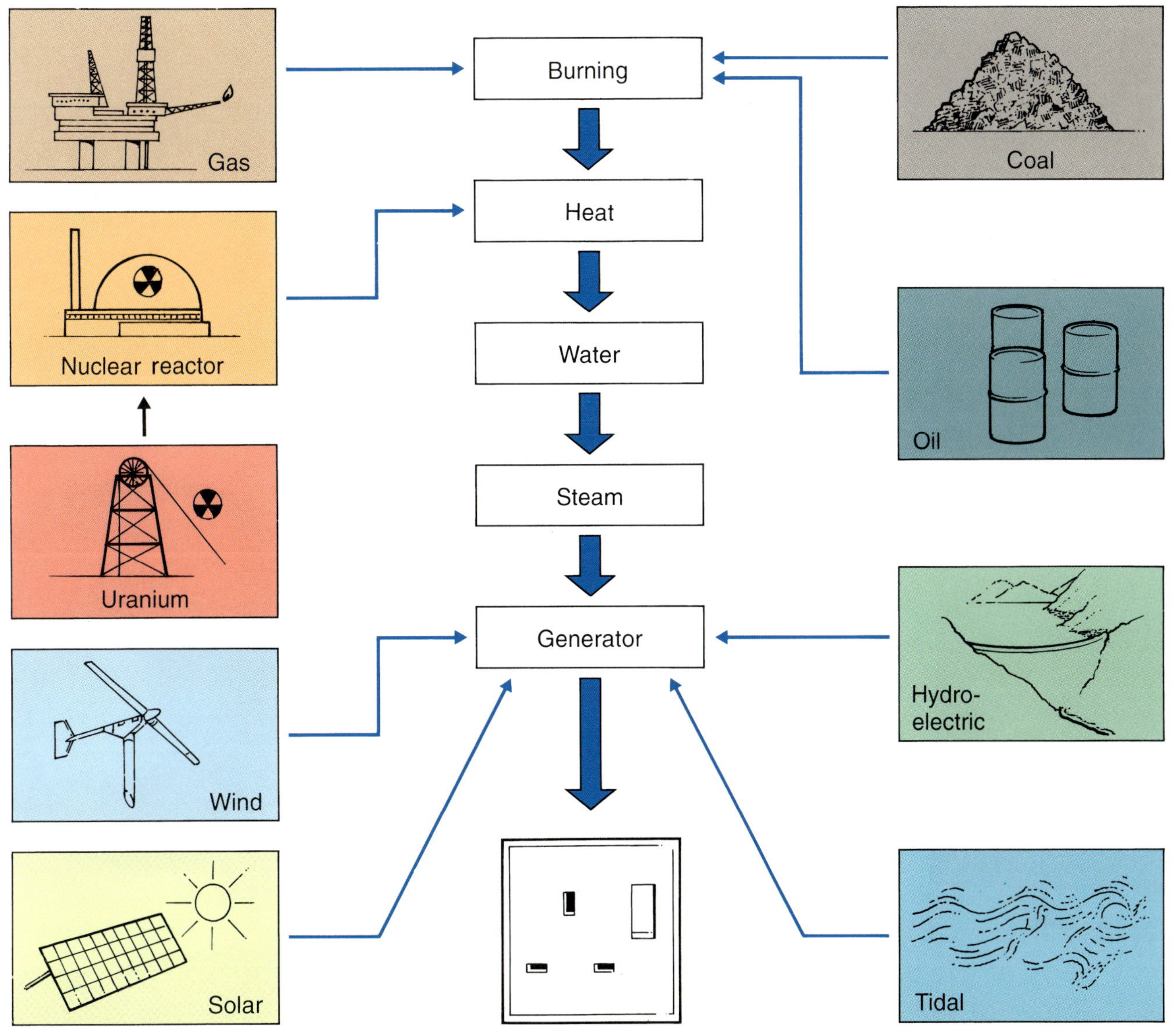

Gas
Nuclear reactor
Uranium
Wind
Solar
Burning
Heat
Water
Steam
Generator
Coal
Oil
Hydro-
electric
Tidal

Tasks

7 List the sources which have to be burned.

8 Which other source produces heat for steam?

9 Sort the sources into those which can be used only once (non renewable) and others which can be used over and over again (renewable).

Renewable	Non-renewable
Solar	Oil

10 Research the polluting effects of heat-producing power stations.

11 Identify the advantages and disadvantages of each source of electricity.

Source	Advantage	Disadvantage
Solar	Free	Less in winter when most electricity needed

PEOPLE AND THE ENVIRONMENT

The Galapagos Islands

There are places in the world which are so important that they need special protection.

The Galapagos Islands are in the Pacific Ocean, 1000 km west of mainland Ecuador. Because they are separated from the mainland, the animal life has developed differently. There are animals on Galapagos which are not found anywhere else. Many of the islands are uninhabited. There are no farm animals or pets such as cats and dogs. These islands were declared wildlife sanctuaries in 1934 and visitors to the islands are still carefully controlled.

Tourists must pay a large fee to enter the islands. Most fly to the only airfield at Baltra Island. From there they travel around the islands by ship. They eat and sleep on the ships. All visitors must be led by a qualified guide and must stay on the pathways.

Tasks

1. Look at the dinghy. Why do the ships not sail to the shore?
2. Describe the ground and vegetation.
3. What would happen if visitors walked wherever they liked?
4. What has been done to protect the land from erosion by walkers?
5. The guide is holding a piece of volcanic rock. Is it light or heavy?
6. Why must tourists have a guide?

The animals are not afraid of people. The visitors only want to shoot cameras not guns.

The male iguana changes colour in the mating season. The Sally Lightfoot crab will scuttle away if a visitor moves but will approach if there is no movement.

The male frigate bird (above) inflates his red pouch in order to attract females. It takes 20 minutes to be full sized. Frigate birds are like flying pirates. They do not hunt their own food. Instead they chase other birds which have made a catch, tug their tail and catch the food which they drop.

Tasks

7 Describe a Sally Lightfoot crab. Is it well camouflaged?

8 Herons catch crabs without flying. They then bang them against the rocks until their legs drop off. Read about how crabs are with people. How do you think the heron catches crabs?

9 What would happen if cats and other pets reached the island?

10 Should visitors be allowed to bring pets along?

11 Why do tourists return to the ship to eat and drink?

12 Why are no hotels being built for them?

13 If you could visit the islands, what would you most like to see?

PEOPLE AND THE ENVIRONMENT

Preserving the rainforests

Tourism can help save the rainforests but it can also change them

People everywhere need jobs. Families need to be fed and better health means more people living longer. In the rainforests this causes conflict. By cutting down trees money can be earned and land made available for crops. If the rainforests are to be saved other work must be found for the people who live there. In the Amazon Rainforests an attempt is being made to keep the forests by encouraging tourists.

Visitors fly to airstrips on the edge of the rainforests. From there they travel by local bus until the forest becomes too dense. The only routes left are the rivers. Local people and tourists transfer to motorised canoes and travel for hours to the depths of the forest.

Tasks

1. Describe the rainforests. How is it different from any forest you have seen in Britain?
2. Describe the weather.
3. Look at the reasons why people go on holiday. List those important to rainforest tourists.

Reasons

Relax
Swim
Sunbathe
Eat and drink
Activity
Learn
Explore
Photography
Dance

Large boats wait up river to carry tourists. The tourists spend some nights on the boat in cabins. Other nights are spent in wooden houses in the rainforest without electricity, toilets or running water.

All people, food, equipment and fuel is carried by canoe.

Tasks

4 Why are rivers so important to rainforest people?

5 Where do you think the empty coke bottle was bought?

6 Describe the rainforest tourist accommodation. Think about design and materials. Why are they built on stilts?

7 Imagine a night spent in one of these houses. Describe what you would most and least enjoy.

8 In the rainforest dead wood rots rapidly. Why is this a problem on the walkways?

9 What jobs does tourism create for local people in the rainforest?

10 What problems might tourism bring?

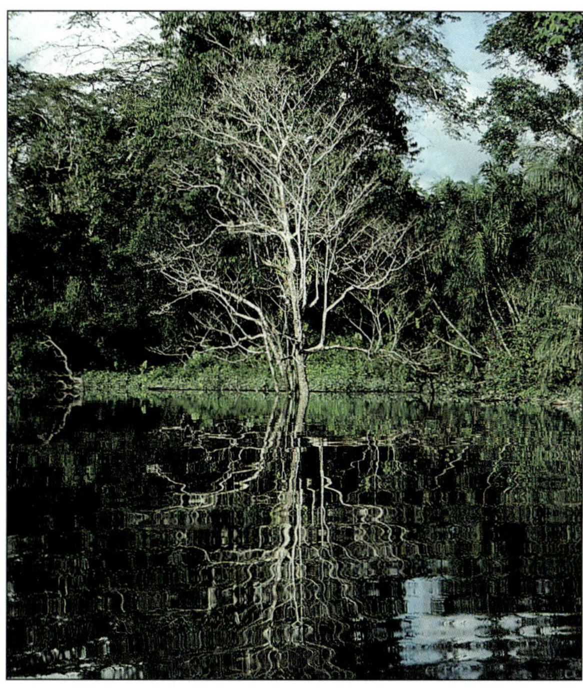

Many tourist journeys through the forest are along specially built wooden walkways.

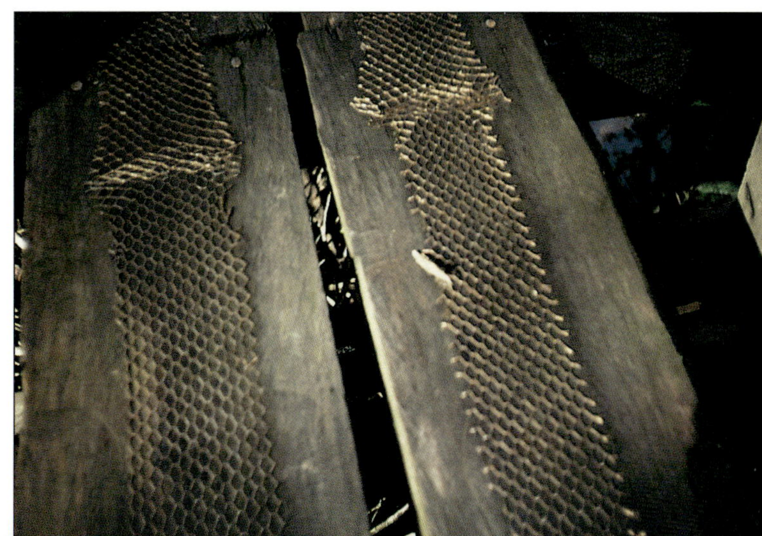

Past beliefs

People's understanding of the shape and size of the earth has changed over time.

From earliest times people have tried to describe and to draw the earth. Their descriptions and maps were based on limited knowledge and scientific guesswork. The Ancient Greeks believed that the sky was supported by Atlas, one of the Titans, but even in those times Pythagoras argued that the world was a globe.

Some Hindus believed that the earth was held up by elephants, whose shiftings caused earthquakes. The elephants stood on a turtle, a form of the god Vishnu, which rested on a cobra, the symbol of water.

Tasks

1. Describe how the Greeks thought of the earth and its place in the Universe.
2. Why would this belief not have appeared silly at the time?
3. How is the name Atlas used today?

In the Middle Ages it was commonly believed that the earth was flat. By the time of Columbus explorers were convinced that the earth was round and sailed west in search of China and India.

Frieslant
Irlant
Hispania
Lisbona
Seville
Marocco
Hair

Tasks

5 If sailors believed the earth was flat would they have felt safer sailing close to shore or far out to sea?

6 What would they fear would happen if they sailed too far from the land?

Look at the old globe.

7 Write the names used for:

a) Spain
b) Lisbon
c) Morocco
d) Ireland

Compare this globe with a modern one.

8 Are the islands west of Africa, Spain and Britain accurate? Describe the differences between the two globes.

9 Why is a modern globe likely to be more accurate?

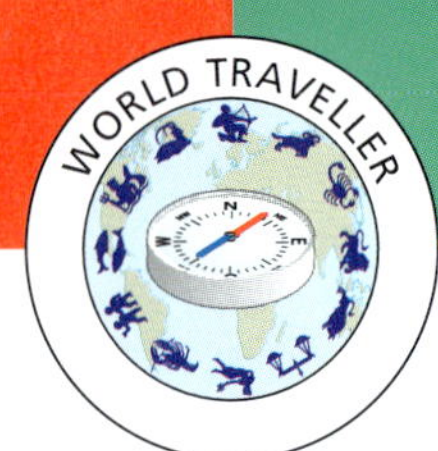
WORLD TRAVELLER

Globes and maps

Flat maps can distort the actual shape of the continents and seas.

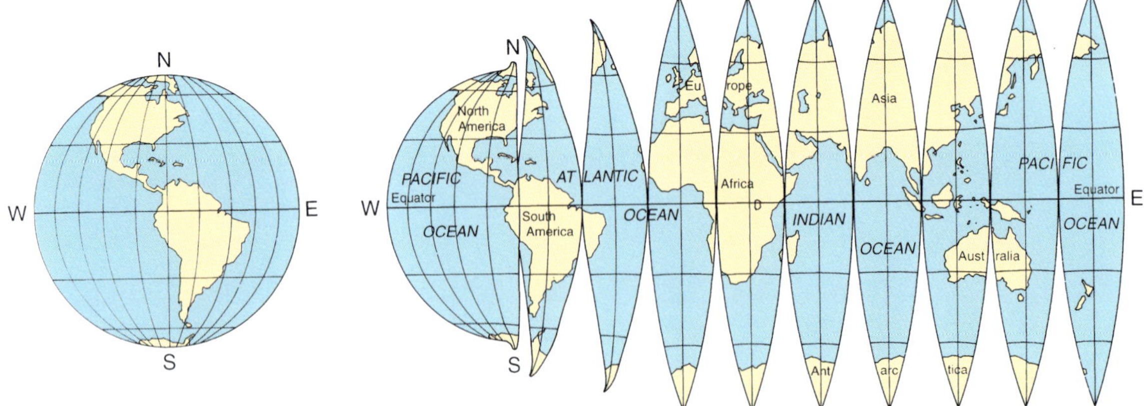
N
W
E
S
North America
PACIFIC
Equator
OCEAN
South America
ATLANTIC
OCEAN
Europe
Africa
INDIAN
OCEAN
Asia
PACIFIC
Equator
OCEAN
Australia
Antarctica

It is very difficult to carry a globe around in your pocket or school bag. It is much easier to draw the world on a flat piece of paper. However by transferring information from a globe to a flat map we change the shape of the land and sea and distances.

Look at Antarctica on the map below. It stretches as far as the whole of North America, Europe and Asia combined. It is not really so large nor is it a long, thin continent. Flat maps distort the shape and size of land more at the Poles than near the Equator.

NORTH POLE
MAP A
ARCTIC OCEAN
Anchorage
CANADA
NORTH
AMERICA
Seattle
Los Angeles
USA
New York
Mississippi R.
ATLANTIC OCEAN
Tropic of Cancer
Oslo
Stockholm
EUROPE
Paris
RUSSIAN FEDERATION
ASIA
Suez Canal
Cairo
HIMALAYAS
INDIA
Beijing
JAPAN
Tokyo
Bombay
R. Nile
AFRICA
THAILAND
PACIFIC OCEAN
Equator
0°
Panama Canal
R. Amazon
BRAZIL
SOUTH
AMERICA
ANDES
PACIFIC OCEAN
Tropic of Capricorn
INDONESIA
INDIAN OCEAN
AUSTRALIA
Sydney
N
Buenos Aires
ATLANTIC OCEAN
Prime meridian
0
3000km
scale at equator
ANTARCTICA
SOUTH POLE

We are so used to looking at flat maps that we begin to think the earth is really as they show it. Try looking at a globe from different angles. The world seems a different place.

Tasks

1 Where is Map A more accurate?

a) Near the River Amazon or the north of Russia?

b) Central Africa or Sydney?

2 Using Map B:

Name the continents, countries, landscape features you would pass over on these routes.

From	To
Oslo	Tokyo
Stockholm	Seattle
Oslo	Los Angeles
Stockholm	Beijing

3 Describe the routes actually flown on Map B.

4 Explain any differences.

The map below shows the earth viewed from above the North Pole. Nothing south of the Equator can be seen.

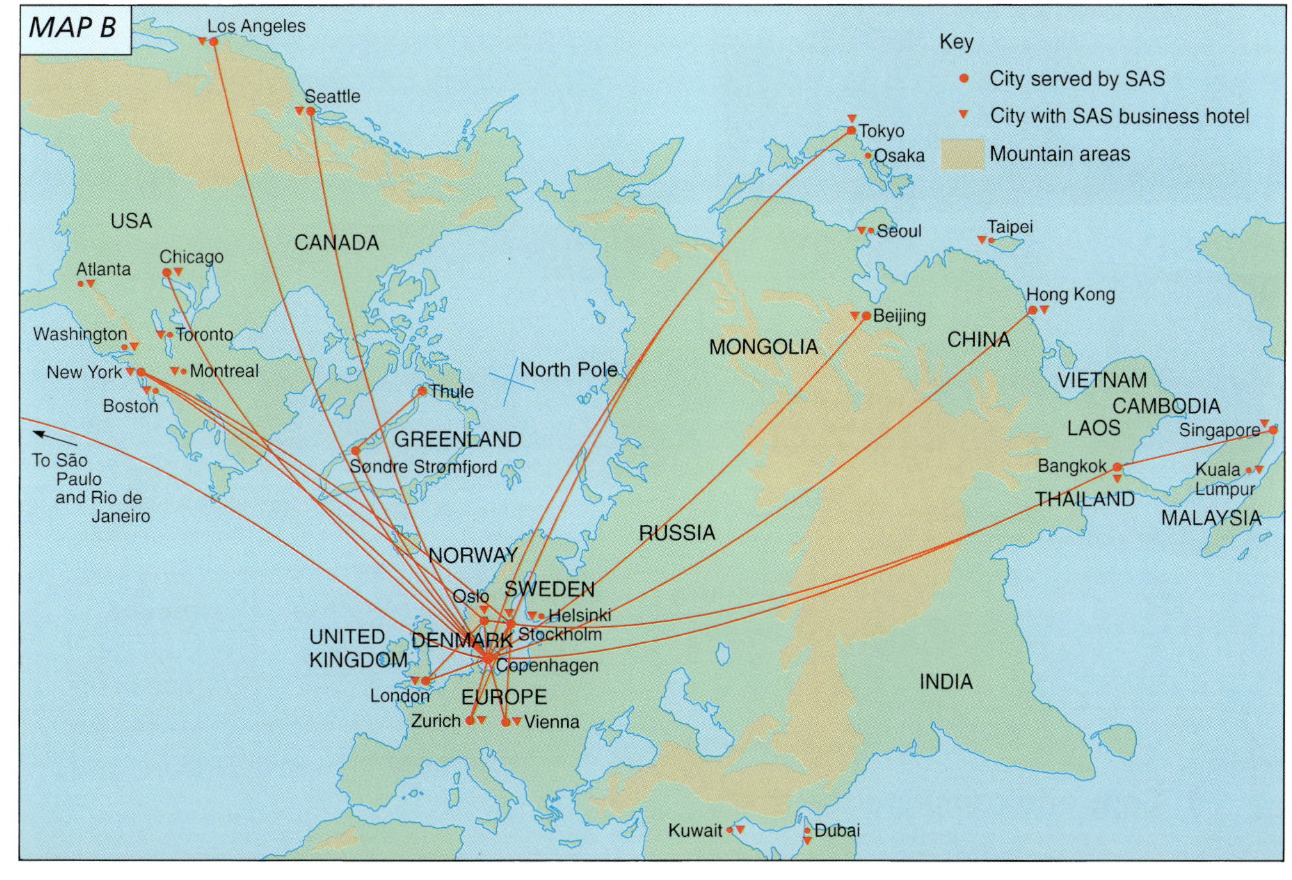
MAP B
Key
City served by SAS
City with SAS business hotel
Mountain areas
Los Angeles
Seattle
USA
CANADA
Atlanta
Chicago
Washington
Toronto
New York
Montreal
Boston
To São Paulo and Rio de Janeiro
Thule
North Pole
GREENLAND
Søndre Strømfjord
NORWAY
Oslo
SWEDEN
Helsinki
Stockholm
UNITED KINGDOM
DENMARK
Copenhagen
London
EUROPE
Zurich
Vienna
RUSSIA
MONGOLIA
Tokyo
Osaka
Seoul
Taipei
Beijing
CHINA
Hong Kong
VIETNAM
CAMBODIA
LAOS
Singapore
Bangkok
THAILAND
Kuala Lumpur
MALAYSIA
INDIA
Kuwait
Dubai

WORLD TRAVELLER

World traveller

An experienced traveller uses maps and globe to plan long journeys.

Most countries of the world have their own currency.

A

100
ΤΡΑΠΕΖΑ ΤΗΣ ΕΛΛΑΔΟΣ
ΔΡΑΧΜΑΙ
ΕΚΑΤΟΝ
27A 358930
100
27A 358930

L

ZWANZIG SCHILLING
OESTERREICHISCHE NATIONALBANK
20
UNITED STATES
VENEZUELA
EIRE
SPAIN

B

10
KYMMENEN
MARKKAA
10
SUOMEN PANKKI
Litt. A
1116165969
1116165969

NEGARA BRUNEI DARUSSALAM
443851
SATU RINGGIT
ONE DOLLAR
443851

C

CENTRAL BANK OF IRELAND
£5
FIVE POUNDS

D

TÜRKIYE CUMHURIYET MERKEZ BANKASI
1000
1000

E

Note	Country	Continent	Currency	Amount
A	Greece	Europe	Drachma	100
B				
C				

Tasks

1 Copy and complete the chart.

FEDERAL RESERVE NOTE
THE UNITED STATES OF AMERICA
THIS NOTE IS LEGAL TENDER FOR ALL DEBTS, PUBLIC AND PRIVATE
B14792434R
WASHINGTON, D.C.
ONE DOLLAR

K

STATE BANK OF PAKISTAN
TEN RUPEES

J

EL BANCO DE ESPAÑA
2Y9938338
CIEN
PESETAS
MADRID, 17 de Noviembre de 1970
100

I

FINLAND
STRIA
TURKEY
EECE
PAKISTAN
INDIA
BRUNEI
MALAYSIA
भारतीय रिज़र्व बैंक
RESERVE BANK OF INDIA
पाँच रुपये
FIVE RUPEES

BANK NEGARA MALAYSIA
SEPULUH RINGGIT
SL4832347
$10

H

F

BANCO CENTRAL DE VENEZUELA
SEPTIEMBRE-21-1989
K16551542
CINCO BOLIVARES

G

Tasks

2 Imagine you have to visit all the countries marked on the map. Plan your journey. Start in Ireland. Try to plan the shortest possible route.

3 Copy and complete a chart like this:

Start	Destination	Direction
Ireland	Spain	south

4 Now carry out the same task using a globe instead of the map.

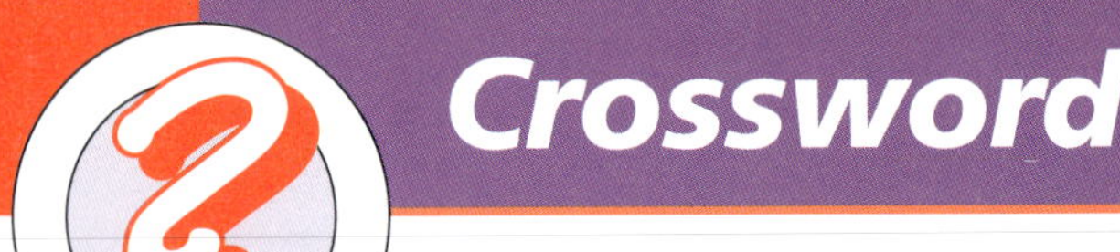

Crossword

How well do you know this book?

Copy and complete the crossword.

To find the answers you will need to look back through this book. Use the contents page to help find the correct section.

Across

1. Country with the world's largest port (11)
7. Best form of transport in rainforest (6)
8. The M25 surrounds it (6)
9. Rupee is the currency (5)
12. Motorway linking London and north-west England (2)
13. Crop grown in Kenya (5)
15. Tributary of the Rhine (4)
18. Land surrounded by water (6)
19. 80% of the people live in rural areas (5)

Down

1. This waste is very dangerous (7)
2. Country south of Kenya (8)
3. Essential but often wasted (11)
4. Name of Greek god who supported the sky (5)
5. Small boat used around the Galapagos Islands (6)
6. A locality north of Nairobi (6, 4)
10. The male changes colour (6)
11. Pythagoras was one (5)
12. Family in Banana Hill (6)
14. River in the Netherlands (4)
16. The North Pole has lots of it (3)
17. Home of the dollar (3)